INTRODUCING
ISSUES WITH
OPPOSING
VIEWPOINTS®

Adoption

Jacqueline Langwith, *Book Editor*

GREENHAVEN PRESS
A part of Gale, Cengage Learning

GALE
CENGAGE Learning·

Detroit • New York • San Francisco • New Haven, Conn • Waterville, Maine • London

Elizabeth Des Chenes, *Director, Content Strategy*
Cynthia Sanner, *Publisher*
Douglas Dentino, *Manager, New Product*

LIBRARY OF CONGRESS CATALOGING-IN-PUBLICATION DATA

Adoption / Jacqueline Langwith, book editor.
     pages cm. -- (Introducing issues with opposing viewpoints)
  Includes bibliographical references and index.
  Audience: Age 14-18.
  Audience: Grade 9-12.
  ISBN 978-0-7377-6918-0 (hardcover)
  1. Adoption--United States--Juvenile literature. 2. Adoption--Juvenile literature.
I. Langwith, Jacqueline.
  HV875.55.A362 2014
  362.7340973--dc23
                                                                2013033191

Printed in the United States of America
1 2 3 4 5 6 7 18 17 16 15 14

Contents

Chapter 3: What Policies Should Govern Adoption?

Foreword

Indulging in a wide spectrum of ideas, beliefs, and perspectives is a critical cornerstone of democracy. After all, it is often debates over differences of opinion, such as whether to legalize abortion, how to treat prisoners, or when to enact the death penalty, that shape our society and drive it forward. Such diversity of thought is frequently regarded as the hallmark of a healthy and civilized culture. As the Reverend Clifford Schutjer of the First Congregational Church in Mansfield, Ohio, declared in a 2001 sermon, "Surrounding oneself with only like-minded people, restricting what we listen to or read only to what we find agreeable is irresponsible. Refusing to entertain doubts once we make up our minds is a subtle but deadly form of arrogance." With this advice in mind, Introducing Issues with Opposing Viewpoints books aim to open readers' minds to the critically divergent views that comprise our world's most important debates.

Introducing Issues with Opposing Viewpoints simplifies for students the enormous and often overwhelming mass of material now available via print and electronic media. Collected in every volume is an array of opinions that captures the essence of a particular controversy or topic. Introducing Issues with Opposing Viewpoints books embody the spirit of nineteenth-century journalist Charles A. Dana's axiom: "Fight for your opinions, but do not believe that they contain the whole truth, or the only truth." Absorbing such contrasting opinions teaches students to analyze the strength of an argument and compare it to its opposition. From this process readers can inform and strengthen their own opinions, or be exposed to new information that will change their minds. Introducing Issues with Opposing Viewpoints is a mosaic of different voices. The authors are statesmen, pundits, academics, journalists, corporations, and ordinary people who have felt compelled to share their experiences and ideas in a public forum. Their words have been collected from newspapers, journals, books, speeches, interviews, and the Internet, the fastest growing body of opinionated material in the world.

Introducing Issues with Opposing Viewpoints shares many of the well-known features of its critically acclaimed parent series, Opposing Viewpoints. The articles are presented in a pro/con format, allowing readers to absorb divergent perspectives side by side. Active reading questions preface each viewpoint, requiring the student to approach the material thoughtfully and carefully. Useful charts, graphs, and cartoons supplement each article. A thorough introduction provides readers with crucial background on an issue. An annotated bibliography points the reader toward articles, books, and websites that contain additional information on the topic. An appendix of organizations to contact contains a wide variety of charities, nonprofit organizations, political groups, and private enterprises that each hold a position on the issue at hand. Finally, a comprehensive index allows readers to locate content quickly and efficiently.

Introducing Issues with Opposing Viewpoints is also significantly different from Opposing Viewpoints. As the series title implies, its presentation will help introduce students to the concept of opposing viewpoints and learn to use this material to aid in critical writing and debate. The series' four-color, accessible format makes the books attractive and inviting to readers of all levels. In addition, each viewpoint has been carefully edited to maximize a reader's understanding of the content. Short but thorough viewpoints capture the essence of an argument. A substantial, thought-provoking essay question placed at the end of each viewpoint asks the student to further investigate the issues raised in the viewpoint, compare and contrast two authors' arguments, or consider how one might go about forming an opinion on the topic at hand. Each viewpoint contains sidebars that include at-a-glance information and handy statistics. A Facts About section located in the back of the book further supplies students with relevant facts and figures.

Following in the tradition of the Opposing Viewpoints series, Greenhaven Press continues to provide readers with invaluable exposure to the controversial issues that shape our world. As John Stuart Mill once wrote: "The only way in which a human being can make some approach to knowing the whole of a subject is by hearing what can be said about it by persons of every variety of opinion and studying all modes in which it can be looked at by every character of mind. No wise man ever acquired his wisdom in any mode but this." It is to this principle that Introducing Issues with Opposing Viewpoints books are dedicated.

Introduction

There are no unwanted children, just unfound families.

—The National Adoption Center

According to data from the US Department of Health and Human Services (HHS), about 250,000 children enter the foster care system every year. These children have generally been removed from their parents' care because of abuse or neglect or because their parents cannot care for them for some reason. Foster care is intended to be a temporary solution until the parents can get back on their feet or another family member is located that can take over care. However, some children will never be reunited with their parents. For these children, adoption provides the only way for them to grow up in a stable family environment.

Children who have been involuntarily removed from the custody of their biological parents and placed in foster care make up the majority of children available for adoption in the United States. The HHS collects national data on foster care children available for adoption. These data show that each year around one hundred thousand children whose parents' parental rights have been terminated are waiting to be adopted. However, only about fifty thousand children are adopted from foster care annually. Approximately twenty-five thousand leave the foster care system each year—not because of adoption, but because they had their eighteenth birthday and aged out of the system. The HHS data show that the typical child waiting for adoption has already been in foster care for three years and is eight years old. The story of a young woman from Florida—Ashley Rhodes-Courter—is reflective of the difficulties facing children in foster care and the benefits of adoption. Ashley's story is provided on the website of AdoptUSkids, an organization sponsored by the US government. Ashley entered the foster care system as a three-year-old when her young mother was arrested for passing bad checks. For the next nine to ten years of her life, Ashley lived in fourteen different foster homes. Some of the homes Ashley was placed in were OK, but others were not. In her story she says that in one foster home "16 foster kids were made to share two bedrooms" and "children were routinely beaten, starved, and locked outside in cold weather."[1]

Ashley was eventually adopted, and it was in her adoptive home that she learned what being in a family was like. Her adoptive parents provided Ashley with positive role models and a loving home in which she thrived. Today Ashley has become a voice for children in foster care. She and her husband have three foster care children, and Ashley has made it her mission to raise awareness about foster care adoption and to reform the system so that foster care children are spared the difficulties she faced. In her narrative, Ashley says, "Even though my story wasn't really ideal, there is still much hope. . . . There are so many misconceptions about who foster and adoptive parents can be and who these kids are. There truly is a kid out there for every family."[2]

The Dave Thomas Foundation for Adoption, a nonprofit adoption advocacy organization, agrees with Ashley. The organization contends that misconceptions and myths prevent many foster care children from finding permanent homes. For instance, according to the foundation, surveys suggest that many Americans believe the myth that children who enter the foster care system have committed a crime. Many people also mistakenly believe that a foster child's biological parent can come to take an adopted child back. Other myths focus on the ability of single people, gay and lesbian couples, or older people to adopt foster care children. The foundation says all of these groups of people can adopt from the foster care system. The foundation contends that these myths prevent foster care adoptions and contribute to tens of thousands of children aging out of the system. According to Rita Soronen, president of the Dave Thomas Foundation for Adoption, children aging out of the system without families of their own "face an uncertain future, filled with higher risks of incarceration, homelessness, early pregnancies, and truncated educations."[3]

To promote the adoption of foster care children, particularly traditionally difficult-to-place foster care children such as older children, those with disabilities or behavioral issues, and children with siblings, the Dave Thomas Foundation for Adoption created the Wendy's Wonderful Kids (WWK) program. The WWK program matches foster care children available for adoption with a recruiter who gets to know them and then actively seeks adoptive parents. An independent research center, Child Trends, studied the WWK approach and found that on average, foster children were 1.7 times more likely to be adopted when these child-focused recruiters helped them find adoptive parents. For difficult-to-place children, the WWK approach is even more effective, according to Child Trends. The approach tripled the rate of adoptions among the most difficult-to-place foster children.

In a story printed in *Adoptive Families* magazine, an adoptive mom to three foster care children, Kate Robertson, provides a poignant description of a foster child waiting for adoption. According to Robertson:

> The faces of waiting children look much the same in every state. They are six and 10 and 12. They are children with difficult histories. They are not infants or toddlers. They are not blank slates. Some have emotional problems and learning disabilities and even serious health concerns. But like all children, they need permanent families. A place to call home, a place of safety and guidance today, a place to bring the grandkids for Christmas tomorrow.[4]

As Robertson writes, foster care children are like any other children; they want a place to call home. In *Introducing Issues with Opposing Viewpoints: Adoption*, the authors provide viewpoints on how adoption should be regarded, the types of adoption that should be encouraged, and the policies that should govern adoption.

Notes

1. Quoted in AdoptUSKids, "Ashley's Story." www.adoptuskids.org /join-the-conversation/real-foster-care-and-adoption-stories/youth -and-foster-alumni/story?k=Ashley-Rhodes.
2. Quoted in AdoptUSKids, "Ashley's Story."
3. Rita Soronen, "'Unadoptable' Is Unacceptable," *RE: Philanthropy* (blog), October 26, 2011. www.cofinteract.org/rephilanthropy/?p=3496.
4. Kate Robertson, "Special Delivery," *Adoptive Families*, 2003. www .adoptivefamilies.com/articles.php?aid=628.

Chapter 1

How Should Adoption Be Viewed?

Adoption is viewed by many as a good option to abortion, but many others disagree.

Adoption Is a Social Good

American Adoptions

American Adoptions is a nonprofit domestic adoption agency that works across the United States. In the following viewpoint the organization claims that adoption is beneficial to at least three groups of people: adoptive parents yearning to have a child, birth mothers who are not ready to be parents at a certain time in their lives, and adopted children who need a safe and loving home.

> "Most of us know at least one person who has benefited from adoption."

AS YOU READ, CONSIDER THE FOLLOWING QUESTIONS:

1. According to American Adoptions, the day a couple chooses adoption signifies the end of what?
2. According to American Adoptions, unintended pregnancies among women in high school or college put a temporary or permanent hold on what?
3. Name three famous people that American Adoptions says were adopted.

The benefits of adoption can be felt by a countless number of people across the United States, as nearly everyone has been touched by adoption in some way. Neighbors, friends, relatives, in-laws—Most of us know at least one person who has benefited from adoption.

While everyone involved in the adoption greatly benefits from adoption, these benefits are unique to each party.

Adoptive Family Benefits

The majority of people work their entire lives to prepare for starting a family one day. However, there are a significant number of couples who, once they reach that point in their lives, are unable to conceive a child due to infertility.

These couples see their lives come to a halt and constantly wonder when they will become pregnant. The couple may seek infertility treatments, which are expensive and can result in drastic physical and emotional changes. For many, the treatments are unsuccessful.

FAST FACT

According to the US Department of Health and Human Services, in 2002 18.5 million women aged eighteen to forty-four (approximately one-third of all American women) had considered adoption at some point in their lives.

Eventually, the couple comes to a decision that all they want is to become parents, and it doesn't matter how.

The day the couple chooses adoption, it signifies the end of their struggles with infertility. It signifies that they are ready and will soon become a mom and dad.

Adoption benefits the couple because they now have a child to share their lives with, to teach right from wrong, and to carry on their name. The child gives the parents a reason to wake up in the morning and to go to bed at night. Everything truly revolves around the child, and the parents often wonder why they waited so long to choose adoption.

For those reasons, the opportunity to experience parenthood is the greatest benefit some couples could ever hope for, which may not have been possible without adoption. . . .

The author asserts that the day a couple chooses to adopt signifies the end of their struggle with infertility and the start of their commitment to becoming parents.

Birth Mother Benefits

Adoption benefits the birth mother as much as anyone, if not more.

For a woman, unexpectedly learning that she is pregnant can be one of the most stressful times she can ever endure. The pregnancy can halt her education, career and other goals she may have. Furthermore, she may not have the finances or a partner in her life to help raise the child, making her situation more difficult.

The woman may be in high school or college when she learns that she is pregnant, and raising the child will undoubtedly put either a temporary or permanent hold on her education. If she doesn't have parents willing to support her or help look after the child, she may struggle balancing one or two jobs while raising the child. Indeed, an unplanned pregnancy can send a woman's life into a tailspin if she doesn't have the proper support system.

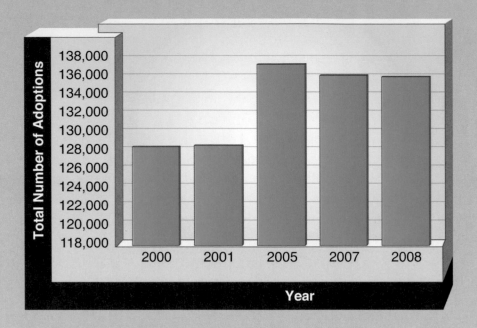

US Adoption Trends, 2000–2008

Total Number of Adoptions

138,000	
136,000	
134,000	
132,000	
130,000	
128,000	
126,000	
124,000	
122,000	
120,000	
118,000	

2000   2001   2005   2007   2008

Year

Taken from: Child Welfare Information Gateway. "How Many Children Were Adopted in 2000–2008?" US Department of Health and Human Services, 2011.

These reasons are why many women selflessly choose adoption for their baby. They may consider raising the child themselves, but women who choose adoption understand that they are not ready to become parents at this time in their lives.

In summation, adoption benefits the birth mother because it grants her a second chance at receiving an education and fulfilling her goals, while ensuring her that her child will be raised in a home with a loving family who have always dreamed of being parents.

For most birth mothers, knowing that their child is safe and happy is the biggest benefit of all. . . .

Adoptee Benefits

What do [country singer] Faith Hill, [civil rights activist] Jesse Jackson, [Apple Inc. cofounder] Steve Jobs, [Wendy's restaurant founder] Dave Thomas, [former president] Gerald Ford and [musician and songwriter] John Lennon all have in common? They, among many other celebrities, were adopted.

How would their lives have turned out if adoption wasn't chosen for them as kids? Would they still have attained stardom? Because these celebrities were placed for adoption, they were given a multitude of opportunities that they may not have otherwise had.

Clearly, not all adopted children will one day become household names, but that doesn't diminish the impact adoption has on a child's opportunities, resulting in a fulfilling and meaningful life.

Simply being provided a safe household and loving parents is a benefit in itself. Adoptive parents are often financially sound as well, so adopted children will be provided the things they need to succeed in life, with the chance to attend college near the top of the list.

But perhaps more importantly is the fact that an adopted child knows she has two parents who love her, as well as a biological mother who loves her so much that she selflessly chose the best life possible for her child. The feeling a child receives knowing that she is loved is immeasurable, and it's obvious a loved child will carry that love and confidence wherever life may take her.

This is truly a benefit that any mother would want for her child.

EVALUATING THE AUTHOR'S ARGUMENTS:

American Adoptions lists adoption benefits to three different groups of people. Can you think of any other groups of people that adoption benefits? Do you think there are any groups of people that may not benefit from adoption?

The Dark Side of Adoptions

Stephanie Pappas

"Research ... found that kids with any institutional rearing had a 53 percent chance of psychiatric disorders compared with 22 percent for kids raised in a home."

The following viewpoint argues that not all adoptions result in happy endings. The author, Stephanie Pappas, explains that there are many factors that are needed for a parent and child to bond. Often newly adopted parents and children expect an immediate bond, but the reality is that developing a relationship with an adopted child is a long process. Adopted children are also more at risk for mental health problems that can disrupt the process of bonding. The risk of adoption disruption increases with age. It is important that potential adoptive parents are aware of the risks and amount of work that goes into adopting a child.

AS YOU READ, CONSIDER THE FOLLOWING QUESTIONS:

1. According to the study cited by the author, what is the name of the emotional disorder parents may experience after adopting a child that is similar to postpartum depression in biological parents?
2. As stated in the viewpoint, what are the rates of failed adoptions in children adopted at infancy, between ages six and eight, and after age fifteen?
3. As attributed to Victor Groza in the viewpoint, what "survival behaviors" do children develop to help them get through bad environments?

I n September 2009, 7-year-old Artyom Savelyev left Russia to live with his new adoptive family in Tennessee. Earlier this month, Artyom returned to Moscow—alone. All he had with him was a backpack and a note penned by Torry Hansen, a 33-year-old nurse and Artyom's adoptive mother.

"I no longer wish to parent this child," read the note, in part. The mother also reportedly said Artyom was mentally unstable.

The case has raised international furor, with Russian authorities suspending adoptions to the United States. It has also drawn attention to a rare but dark side of adoption: What happens when the bond between adoptive parents and children doesn't form.

Building a Bond

Even for biological parents, bonding is complex. The hormone oxytocin, which induces maternal behavior in animals, helps to facilitate the attachment between mother and child.

But hormones are only part of the story. Attachments take time, and postpartum depression or other mental health problems can disrupt the process.

Bonding with adoptive children is similar. Some parents feel an immediate emotional connection, while others struggle for months or years. A study last month [March 2010] in the *Western Journal of Nursing Research* found that adoptive parents can experience "post-adoption depression" when their expectations about the adoption experience aren't met. These parents often report difficulty bonding with the child.

Disrupted Adoptions

While bonding may be slow, most adoptions work out. According to a review of American adoptions in the book *Clinical and Practice Issues in Adoption* (Greenwood Publishing Group, 1998), 80 percent of placements make it to legalization. After the paperwork is in, the success rate was 98 percent.

But in extreme cases, the adoption "disrupts," and the child is sent back to the agency or foster home. This process is rarely as dramatic as Artyom's unaccompanied flight from Washington, D.C., to Moscow, but the case matches previous research in other ways. The risk of adoption disruption increases with age, from less than 1 percent in

Studies show that nearly 40 percent of mothers who give up their babies for adoption report depression.

infants to up to 26 percent for kids adopted after age 15, according two 1988 studies.

The second of those studies, published in the journal *Social Work,* found a disruption rate of 10 percent for children adopted between the ages of 6 and 8. Artyom was 7 when he came to America.

Orphanage Drawbacks

Artyom's childhood in a Russian orphanage may also have put him at risk. Research on children in Romanian orphanages found that kids with any institutional rearing had a 53 percent chance of psychiatric disorders compared with 22 percent for kids raised in a home. The study, published in 2009 in the *American Journal of Psychiatry,* also found that children randomly assigned to move out of an orphanage into foster care had rates of anxiety and depression half those of children who stayed in the orphanage.

When it comes to getting kids out of institutions, "the younger the better," said Charles Zeanah, a child and adolescent psychiatrist at Tulane University and author of the 2009 research article. "The less exposure to the institutional environment, the better chance that the kid is going to look better down the road."

Institutions often feature overburdened caregivers who work in shifts, Zeanah said. These caregivers can't bond with every child, and the children don't spend enough time with them to form attachments. Overcoming the effects of that environment can take years of hard work.

"Kids develop what we call survival behaviors," said Victor Groza, a professor of parent-child studies at Case Western Reserve University in Ohio. Aggression and violence can help kids survive in bad environments, Groza said, and kids "do not let go of those behaviors automatically."

Making Adoptions Work

Artyom's adoptive grandmother told the Associated Press that the boy exhibited many of these behaviors, including violent tantrums and attempts to set fires. But the boy was never evaluated by a mental health professional. Multiple studies in the 1980s and 1990s found

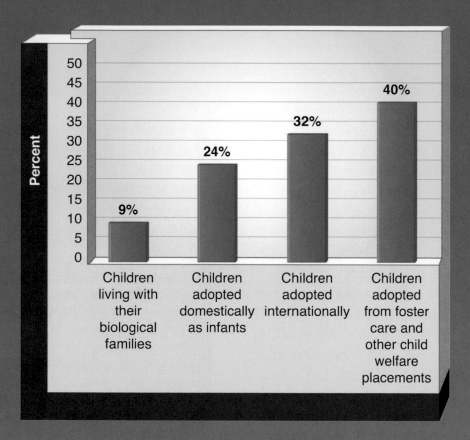

Percent of Birth Children and Adopted Children Receiving Special Education Services

Percent

- 50
- 45
- 40 — 40%
- 35 — 32%
- 30
- 25 — 24%
- 20
- 15
- 10 — 9%
- 5
- 0

Children living with their biological families

Children adopted domestically as infants

Children adopted internationally

Children adopted from foster care and other child welfare placements

Taken from: Evan B. Donaldson Adoption Institute. "Adoption in the Schools: A Lot to Learn," 2006. Reporting data from J. Howard, S. Smith, and S. Ryan. "A Comparative Study of Child Welfare Adoption with Other Types of Adopted Children and Birth Children." *Adoption Quarterly*, 2004.

that behavioral problems were a risk factor for disrupted adoptions, as was the parents' lack of flexibility in dealing with the behavior.

The key to successful adoptions is parental expectation, Groza said. Agencies must be sure that parents really understand the child's needs, and they must follow up with families who are struggling. Parents must understand that their child may need help, and they must be willing to delay gratification and reach out for support, Groza added.

"The likelihood is, things are not going to be bad, but you have to make sure that you have a plan and have gone through, 'What if this comes up, what if that comes up?'" he said.

It's a familiar strategy to Don Harris of Gilford, N.H., who adopted his daughters Molly and Hanna as babies from China. Hanna, now 10, turned out to have speech development problems and other special needs, likely as a result of sensory and nutritional deficiencies in the first 20 months of her life.

People have often asked "in a tactful sort of way," whether he would have adopted Hanna if he'd known how much help she'd need, Harris said. His answer is always the same: "Of course." He felt a bond within 24 hours of meeting Hanna, and the little girl—with her love of seashells, the color brown and hot-and-sour soup—has brought more joy into his life than he could have imagined.

"When you decide that you're going to adopt a child, it's a journey of faith," Harris said. "You need to understand why you're doing it, and you have to have a tremendous amount of faith that the referral that ends up in your hands was meant to be there."

EVALUATING THE AUTHOR'S ARGUMENTS:

Viewpoint author Stephanie Pappas cites personal examples, studies, and statistics to support her contention that adoption can be harmful. Which of these do you think is the most reliable in general and specifically in Pappas's viewpoint, and why?

International Adoption Can Help Children in Other Countries

"For children who have no home, no family willing or able to care for them, or no realistic in-country permanent care option, intercountry adoption may represent their only chance for a safe, loving, permanent family of their own."

National Council for Adoption

In the following viewpoint the National Council for Adoption (NCFA) maintains that intercountry, or international, adoption is necessary to help children around the world. The NCFA says that those who want to eliminate international adoption based on cultural considerations can provide no alternative other than to condemn orphans to life in an institution. This is destructive, says the NCFA; all children deserve a loving and permanent home. The NCFA is a nonprofit organization that promotes infant, intercountry, and foster care adoption.

AS YOU READ, CONSIDER THE FOLLOWING QUESTIONS:
  1. According to the NCFA, in what year did intercountry adoptions peak?
  2. What does the Hague Convention on Intercountry Adoption provide, according to the NCFA?
  3. Whom does the NCFA call on to expand its missions to include permanency options for institutionalized children by promoting intercountry adoption?

The U.S. Department of State has just [November 2011] released the intercountry adoption numbers for FY [fiscal year] 2011.... In 2011, 9,320 children from foreign countries were adopted by U.S. citizens. This represents a 15% decrease in the number of intercountry adoptions from FY 2010.

The number of intercountry adoptions peaked in 2004, when American families adopted more than 22,000 foreign-born children. Since then, however, the number of children adopted each year via intercountry adoption has steadily declined.

Declines in International Adoptions Are Not Good for Children

"This trend is not right, and it is not good for children. Given the increasing number of orphaned children worldwide, the continued decline in intercountry adoptions means that children's most basic needs and rights are being denied," says Chuck Johnson, president and CEO of the National Council For Adoption (NCFA). "As intercountry adoption programs close or decrease in number, more and more children remain in institutions and temporary care situations, aging out without ever securing their basic right to a permanent loving family of their own."

It is important to acknowledge and work together to address legitimate issues of concern in intercountry adoption. Abuse and fraud in the adoption process should always be condemned whenever and wherever they occur, and it is the responsibility of all governments, child welfare workers, and adoption advocates to work to prevent such abuses. However, adoption process abuses are the exception and not the rule, and should not be exaggerated at the expense of the millions of children who still await love, safety, and permanency.

The Hague Convention on Intercountry Adoption has provided both sending and receiving countries with guidelines in support of an ethical, more transparent intercountry adoption system that adheres to international standards. The Hague Convention is also intended to facilitate and promote adoptions for children in need of families; however, in practice, this does not always occur.

Many who oppose intercountry adoption due to national or cultural considerations offer no viable alternative for orphaned, abandoned, and vulnerable children, other than a continuation of the status quo. This is why it is critical for governments, non-governmental organizations, child welfare advocates, and international aid organizations to recognize and uphold the child's right to a family as early in life as possible.

FAST FACT

According to the US Department of State, girls are adopted internationally about 1.7 times more often than boys; 141,321 girls and 83,291 boys were adopted internationally from 1999 to 2011.

"We do not deny the importance of ethnic, cultural, or national identity," says Johnson, "but extensive research, common sense, and our human compassion all tell us that children need more than food and shelter and mere survival. They also need and deserve love, security, and purpose—something that can only be provided by a permanent, loving family, which institutional care or other temporary alternatives can never provide even with the best of intentions.

Children Need and Deserve a Permanent Home

"We call on UNICEF [United Nations Chidren's Fund] and other international aid organizations to expand their missions to include real and timely permanency options for children in institutional care, by advocating more strongly and proactively for intercountry adoption. Those who want better outcomes for all children, especially those who have been orphaned, cannot realize this goal without strengthening and

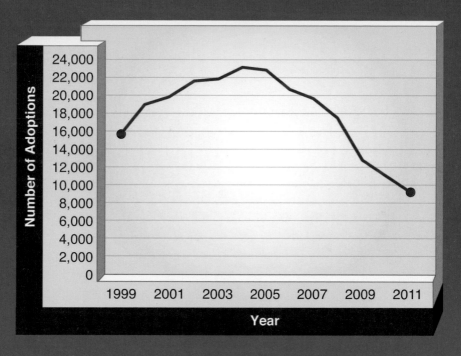

Adoptions into the United States from Other Countries, 1999–2011

Number of Adoptions

24,000
22,000
20,000
18,000
16,000
14,000
12,000
10,000
8,000
6,000
4,000
2,000
0

1999 2001 2003 2005 2007 2009 2011

Year

supporting legal, ethical adoption as [a] means of providing children with the permanent families that they need and deserve."

All child welfare advocates have the responsibility to work to prevent family dissolution and child abandonment whenever possible. Also, when possible, families should receive the support and services they need in order to remain together. In parallel, domestic and international adoption programs should also be encouraged and supported, so that children in need of permanent care have the option of an adoptive placement as early in life as possible.

"For children who have no home, no family willing or able to care for them, or no realistic in-country permanent care option, intercountry adoption may represent their only chance for a safe, loving, permanent family of their own," says Frank Garrott, president and CEO of The Gladney Center for Adoption.

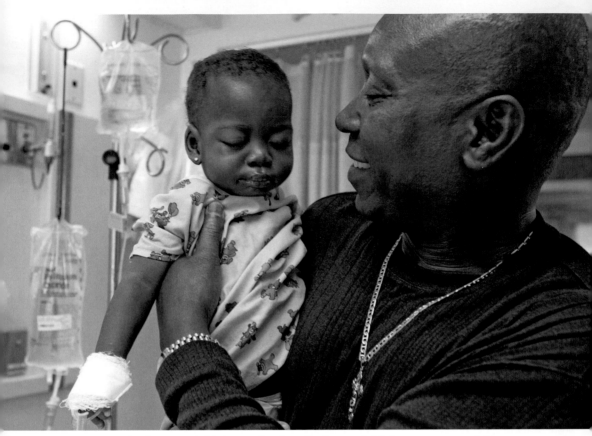

A Cleveland, Ohio, man holds his newly adopted Liberian child. In 2011, 9,320 children from foreign countries were adopted into US families.

"Tragically, too many of these children will never realize their intrinsic right to a family," says Bill Rosen, an NCFA Board Member and Chairman of the Intercountry Adoption Committee. "Too many will move from temporary placement to temporary placement, or spend all their young lives in institutional care. Too many will experience great hardship, loneliness, abuse, inadequate nutrition, poor healthcare, and substandard education in underfunded and understaffed orphanages. Too many will then age out of the system with no real home and no family, ill equipped to support themselves and overcome the enormous challenges they face."

International Adoption Is Necessary

Numerous studies have clearly proven the destructive effects of institutionalization on the physical, emotional, and mental wellbeing of children. Yet for many orphaned and abandoned children worldwide, an orphanage is the only "home" they will ever know.

In contrast, studies of adopted children have shown the tremendous benefits of adoption for children's overall health, development, sense of security, and long-term outcomes. Given the large and increasing number of children in need of care who deserve permanency, intercountry adoption must remain an important part of a complete, holistic, child-centered welfare policy.

EVALUATING THE AUTHOR'S ARGUMENTS:

After reading the viewpoint that follows, by Michele B. Goodwin, how adequately do you think the author of this viewpoint, National Council for Adoption, addresses some of the arguments against international adoptions?

Viewpoint

4

*"Adoption
has become
a cottage
industry,
where
children are
exploited and
sometimes
are not truly
surrendered
for
adoption."*

International Adoption Does Not Always Help Children in Other Countries

Michele B. Goodwin

In the following viewpoint Michele B. Goodwin argues that international adoptions are not always good for children. Goodwin discusses the case of Justin Hansen, a seven-year-old boy whose adoptive US mother sent him back to Russia, alone; she contended he was psychologically damaged and she could no longer care for him. Goodwin says that Justin's case is indicative of a system beset by fraud and abuse in which children are exploited and treated like commodities. Adoptive parents are also taken advantage of, says Goodwin. They spend tens of thousands of dollars and are often lied to by international adoption agencies, she says. Goodwin is a professor of law and medicine at the University of Minnesota. She is the author of *Baby Markets: Money and the New Politics of Creating Families.*

Michele B. Goodwin, "Questioning International Adoptions," *New York Times* online, April 12, 2010.
NYTimes.com. Copyright © 2010 by Michele B. Goodwin. All rights reserved. Reproduced by permission.

More than 30 years ago, Elisabeth Landes and Prof. Richard Posner, now a federal appellate court judge, warned that there was "a considerable amount of baby selling" happening in the United States. Not surprisingly, this daunting assessment attracted strident criticism. Lawyers, social workers and others claimed that the article, which became euphemistically known as the "baby-selling article," overstated the case and surmised that what they observed were necessary transaction fees attached to adoptions and nothing more. But the article's observation sheds light on the case of Justin Hansen, the little boy who was adopted by an American woman and then returned to a Russian orphanage last week [April 2010].

Buying and Selling of Children

The case of Justin and his adoption by an American woman living with her mother has caused considerable controversy and evoked scrutiny from many countries. Some commentators claim that the boy simply had attachment disorder and that his adoptive grandmother, Nancy Hansen, and mother, Torry Hansen, should have tried harder with therapy. Others are sympathetic with the Hansens, who claim that the boy was violent, often had tantrums and threatened to burn down their home.

But this case is far more complicated than what many people understand. International adoptions have become a cottage industry. Americans are the leading importers of children in need of adoption. As the American demand for children from abroad has grown, the supply has been provided by a range of agencies—some legitimate

Documents of children awaiting adoption sit at the National Adoption Council in Guatemala City, Guatemala. The council created a registry in 2008 to help prevent fraud in Guatemala's adoption process.

and others quite questionable. At the same time, the costs and special transaction fees associated with international adoptions have risen.

In effect, the dynamics of law and economics are at play, with the costs of adopting children from abroad rising each year. Some critics of international adoption point out that adoption has become a cottage industry, where children are exploited and sometimes are not truly surrendered for adoption.

David Smolin, a law professor, counts himself as being in this unusual space. When he arranged to adopt two girls from India in the late '90s, he believed that his new daughters were orphaned. After they arrived, he soon discovered that the girls were never surrendered for adoption, but were basically trafficked—stolen from their mother. In addition, the most painful part for his daughters was that the agency lied about their ages. As it turned out, they were older than the documents claimed they were.

But Smolin's case is not unique. Other families face similar traumas and uncomfortable revelations. Maria Melichar of Mayer, Minn., spent $30,000 to adopt two girls from India, Komal and her sister, Shallu. After they arrived, the girls, who had been described as ages 12 and 11 respectively, had difficulty adjusting to their new American surroundings. Komal was often violent and angry. The family soon learned why, but not before spending tens of thousands of dollars and expending considerable energy to support their new daughters. In a shocking revelation, the parents learned that their new daughters were actually 21 and 15.

Everyone had been exploited; the girls and the Minnesota couple. In that case, too, the girls were sent back home.

Children Are Victimized, Not Rescued

Adoption fraud makes international adoptions a far more complicated zone. For decades, psychologists and others have described the tensions and unhappiness that children experience after their placement as "attachment disorder." Surely in many cases they are right. But there are times when the label does not apply and can be misleading. This is compounded by language barriers; Americans adopt children from Russia, China, Korea, Guatemala and other countries without any language proficiencies in their children's native tongues and therefore cannot communicate effectively.

FAST FACT

On December 28, 2012, a Russian law was enacted banning US citizens from adopting Russian children.

Conflating all cases of adoptees not adapting well as "attachment disorder" obscures the fact that agencies and orphanages with very murky practices have rapidly developed in places like Russia, Guatemala, India, and other countries—to ship kids to the United States because it is profitable.

For children stolen from their parents, or trafficked for some other reason, the anxiety displayed may be because they feel victimized, not rescued from their circumstances. In fact, Guatemala, a country that ranks among the top four in the number of children sent to the United States for adoption, recently clamped down out of fear that children were being stolen from their parents, exploited in sex rings and trafficked for their organs. This was a powerful statement coming

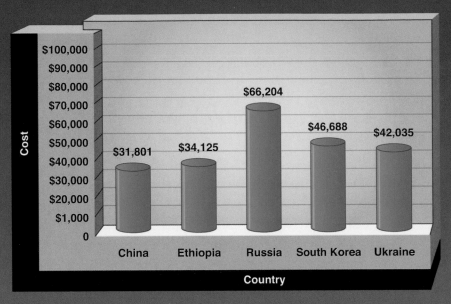

Average International Adoption Cost, 2010–2011

Taken from: "Cost and Timing of Adoption Survey 2010/2011." *Adoptive Families Magazine*, 2013. www.adoptivefamilies.com/articles.php?aid=2350.

from a nation where one child for every hundred ends up in a United States home.

The case of Justin Hansen and his would-be American family highlights contemporary fault lines in international adoptions. Sometimes not all adoptions are exactly what they appear to be.

EVALUATING THE AUTHOR'S ARGUMENTS:

Statistics, anecdotes, and quotations are among the types of evidence writers can use to support their viewpoint. What type(s) of evidence does Michele Goodwin use? Do you think she effectively supports her viewpoint?

Chapter 2

What Types of Adoption Should Be Encouraged?

Controversy has arisen over adoption by same-sex couples, as well as over transracial adoption.

Same-Sex-Couple Adoption Should Be Encouraged

"Gay parents may bring talents to the table that straight parents don't."

Stephanie Pappas

In the following viewpoint Stephanie Pappas asserts that children with gay parents are well adjusted and fare no differently than children with heterosexual parents in mental health, social functioning, and other measures. According to Pappas, same-sex couples tend to be more motivated to adopt and more committed to being good parents, because generally they choose to be parents. The only disadvantage that children of same-sex couples experience, says Pappas, is the discrimination and rejection of their parents by society. Pappas is a senior writer for LiveScience, a website that provides science, health, and technology information.

AS YOU READ, CONSIDER THE FOLLOWING QUESTIONS:
1. What percentage of gay and lesbian couples adopted across races, according to the 2011 report by the Evan B. Donaldson Adoption Institute mentioned in the viewpoint?
2. Why does sociologist Judith Stacey speculate that gay men will be the best parents on average, according to the author?
3. According to the study published in the *Journal of Marriage and Family*, cited by Pappas, how many teenagers and young adults with gay parents rejected the right of gays and lesbians to marry?

G ay marriage, and especially gay parenting, has been in the cross hairs in recent days.

On Jan. 6 [2012], Republican presidential hopeful Rick Santorum told a New Hampshire audience that children are better off with a father in prison than being raised in a home with lesbian parents and no father at all. And last Monday (Jan. 9 [2012]), Pope Benedict called gay marriage a threat "to the future of humanity itself," citing the need for children to have heterosexual homes.

But research on families headed by gays and lesbians doesn't back up these due assertions. In fact, in some ways, gay parents may bring talents to the table that straight parents don't.

Gay parents "tend to be more motivated, more committed than heterosexual parents on average, because they chose to be parents," said Abbie Goldberg, a psychologist at Clark University in Massachusetts who researches gay and lesbian parenting. Gays and lesbians rarely become parents by accident, compared with an almost 50 percent accidental pregnancy rate among heterosexuals, Goldberg said. "That translates to greater commitment on average and more involvement."

And while research indicates that kids of gay parents show few differences in achievement, mental health, social functioning and other measures, these kids may have the advantage of open-mindedness, tolerance and role models for equitable relationships, according to some research. Not only that, but gays and lesbians are likely to provide homes for difficult-to-place children in the foster system, studies show. . . .

Adopting the Neediest

Gay adoption recently caused controversy in Illinois, where Catholic Charities adoption services decided in November [2011] to cease offering services because the state refused funding unless the groups agreed not to discriminate against gays and lesbians. Rather than comply, Catholic Charities closed up shop.

Catholic opposition aside, research suggests that gay and lesbian parents are actually a powerful resource for kids in need of adoption. According to a 2007 report by the Williams Institute and the Urban Institute, 65,000 kids were living with adoptive gay parents between 2000 and 2002, with another 14,000 in foster homes headed by gays and lesbians. (There are currently more than 100,000 kids in foster care in the U.S.)

An October 2011 report by Evan B. Donaldson Adoption Institute found that, of gay and lesbian adoptions at more than 300 agencies, 10 percent of the kids placed were older than 6—typically a very difficult age to adopt out. About 25 percent were older than 3. Sixty percent of gay and lesbian couples adopted across races, which is important given that minority children in the foster system tend to linger. More than half of the kids adopted by gays and lesbians had special needs.

The report didn't compare the adoption preferences of gay couples directly with those of heterosexual couples, said author David Brodzinsky, research director at the Institute and co-editor of *Adoption By Lesbians and Gay Men: A New Dimension of Family Diversity* (Oxford University Press, 2011). But research suggests that gays and lesbians are more likely than heterosexuals to adopt older, special-needs and minority children, he said. Part of that could be their own preferences, and part could be because of discrimination by adoption agencies that puts more difficult children with what caseworkers see as "less desirable" parents.

No matter how you slice it, Brodzinsky told LiveScience, gays and lesbians are highly interested in adoption as a group. The 2007 report by the Urban Institute also found that more than half of gay men and 41 percent of lesbians in the U.S. would like to adopt. That adds up to an estimated 2 million gay people who are interested in adoption. It's a huge reservoir of potential parents who could get kids out of the instability of the foster system, Brodzinsky said.

"When you think about the 114,000 children who are freed for adoption who continue to live in foster care and who are not being readily adopted, the goal is to increase the pool of available, interested and well-trained individuals to parent these children," Brodzinsky said.

In addition, Brodzinsky said, there's evidence to suggest that gays and lesbians are especially accepting of open adoptions, where the child retains some contact with his or her birth parents. And the statistics bear out that birth parents often have no problem with their kids being raised by same-sex couples, he added.

"Interestingly, we find that a small percentage [of birth mothers], but enough to be noteworthy, make a conscious decision to place with gay men, so they can be the only mother in their child's life," Brodzinsky said.

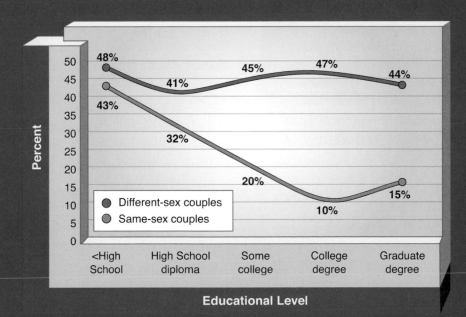

Same-Sex Couples Raising Children Tend to Have Lower Educational Attainment than Different-Sex Couples

Based on data from the US Census American Community Survey, 2009.

Taken from: Gary J. Gates. "Family Formation and Raising Children Among Same-Sex Couples." *NCFR Report,* Winter 2011.

Good Parenting

Research has shown that the kids of same-sex couples—both adopted and biological kids—fare no worse than the kids of straight couples on mental health, social functioning, school performance and a variety of other life-success measures.

In a 2010 review of virtually every study on gay parenting, New York University sociologist Judith Stacey and University of Southern California sociologist Tim Biblarz found no differences between children raised in homes with two heterosexual parents and children raised with lesbian parents.

"There's no doubt whatsoever from the research that children with two lesbian parents are growing up to be just as well-adjusted and successful as children with a male and a female parent," Stacey told LiveScience.

> **FAST FACT**
>
> African Americans in same-sex couples are 2.4 times more likely than their white counterparts to be raising children (40 percent versus 16 percent, respectively), according to analyses of data from the US Census Bureau's American Community Survey from 2005–2009.

There is very little research on the children of gay men, so Stacey and Biblarz couldn't draw conclusions on those families. But Stacey suspects that gay men "will be the best parents on average," she said.

That's a speculation, she said, but if lesbian parents have to really plan to have a child, it's even harder for gay men. Those who decide to do it are thus likely to be extremely committed, Stacey said. Gay men may also experience fewer parenting conflicts, she added. Most lesbians use donor sperm to have a child, so one mother is biological and the other is not, which could create conflict because one mother may feel closer to the kid.

"With gay men, you don't have that factor," she said. "Neither of them gets pregnant, neither of them breast-feeds, so you don't have that asymmetry built into the relationship."

The bottom line, Stacey said, is that people who say children need both a father and a mother in the home are misrepresenting the research, most of which compares children of single parents to children of married

Sixty percent of gay and lesbian couples adopt outside their race, and more than half adopt children with special needs.

couples. Two good parents are better than one good parent, Stacey said, but one good parent is better than two bad parents. And gender seems to make no difference. While you do find broad differences between how men and women parent on average, she said, there is much more diversity within the genders than between them.

"Two heterosexual parents of the same educational background, class, race and religion are more like each other in the way they parent than one is like all other women and one is like all other men," she said.

Nurturing Tolerance

In fact, the only consistent places you find differences between how kids of gay parents and kids of straight parents turn out are in issues of tolerance and open-mindedness, according to Goldberg. In a paper published in 2007 in the *American Journal of Orthopsychiatry*, Goldberg conducted in-depth interviews with 46 adults with at least one gay parent. Twenty-eight of them spontaneously offered that they felt more open-minded and empathetic than people not raised in their situation.

"These individuals feel like their perspectives on family, on gender, on sexuality have largely been enhanced by growing up with gay parents," Goldberg said.

One 33-year-old man with a lesbian mother told Goldberg, "I feel I'm a more open, well-rounded person for having been raised in a non-traditional family, and I think those that know me would agree. My mom opened me up to the positive impact of differences in people."

Children of gay parents also reported feeling less stymied by gender stereotypes than they would have been if raised in straight households. That's likely because gays and lesbians tend to have more egalitarian relationships than straight couples, Goldberg said. They're also less wedded to rigid gender stereotypes themselves.

"Men and women felt like they were free to pursue a wide range of interests," Goldberg said. "Nobody was telling them, 'Oh, you can't do that, that's a boy thing,' or 'That's a girl thing.'"

Same-Sex Acceptance

If same-sex marriage does disadvantage kids in any way, it has nothing to do with their parent's gender and everything to do with society's reaction toward the families, said Indiana University sociologist Brian Powell, the author of *Counted Out: Same-Sex Relations and Americans' Definitions of Family* (Russell Sage Foundation, 2010).

"Imagine being a child living in a state with two parents in which, legally, only one parent is allowed to be their parent," Powell told LiveScience. "In that situation, the family is not seen as authentic or real by others. That would be the disadvantage."

In her research, Goldberg has found that many children of gay and lesbian parents say that more acceptance of gay and lesbian families, not less, would help solve this problem.

In a study published online Jan. 11, 2012, in the *Journal of Marriage and Family*, Goldberg interviewed another group of 49 teenagers and young adults with gay parents and found that not one of them rejected the right of gays and lesbians to marry. Most cited legal benefits as well as social acceptance.

"I was just thinking about this with a couple of friends and just was in tears thinking about how different my childhood might have been had same-sex marriage been legalized 25 years ago," a 23-year-old man raised by a lesbian couple told Goldberg. "The cultural, legal status of same-sex couples impacts the family narratives of same-sex families—how we see ourselves in relation to the larger culture, whether we see ourselves as accepted or outsiders."

EVALUATING THE AUTHOR'S ARGUMENTS:

How many different sources of information does Stephanie Pappas use to support her viewpoint? Do you think her sources are credible? What types of factors did you consider when you assessed the credibility of Pappas's sources?

Is Gay Parenting Bad for the Kids?

Charles C.W. Cooke

"Children with a parent in a same-sex relationship 'underperform' in almost every category."

In the following viewpoint Charles C.W. Cooke contends that children of same-sex couples experience disadvantages that children of heterosexual couples do not. Cooke points to a large study conducted by sociologist Mark Regnerus, which he says contradicts claims that children raised by same-sex couples fare no differently than children raised by heterosexual couples. According to Regnerus's study, says Cooke, children raised by same-sex parents are more likely to experience sexual abuse, spend time in foster care, get arrested, and face many other difficulties. Cooke is an editorial associate for *National Review*, a conservative newsmagazine.

AS YOU READ, CONSIDER THE FOLLOWING QUESTIONS:
1. According to Cooke, what is the source of the "famous" declaration that two women parent better on average than a woman and a man?
2. How many people did Regnerus screen for the study, as cited by Cooke? From these, how many were raised for *some* of their childhood by a mother in a lesbian relationship, and how many were raised for *some* of their childhood by a father in a gay relationship?
3. According to Cooke, given the way the study is set up, it is not so much an analysis of homosexual parenting versus heterosexual parenting, but an analysis of what?

In his new *Social Science Journal* study, Mark Regnerus poses a question: "How different are the adult children of parents who have same-sex relationships?" The answer to this—in both the academic literature and the imagination of the American public—has changed dramatically in less than a generation. "Fifteen years ago," Regnerus explained at an event at the nonpartisan Institute for American Values, biological, heterosexual families were "reflexively regarded as the best environment for children." This subsequently gave way to the notion that there were "no meaningful differences" in outcomes for children raised in non-traditional arrangements. Finally it was suggested that children "might actually be better off being raised by a gay couple."

Although there is little hard evidence to support such a conclusion, advocates of same-sex marriage and gay adoption have declared the science to be settled. Most famous, perhaps, of such declarations is the 2010 paper by social scientists Judith Stacey and Timothy Biblarz, who contended that "based strictly on the published science, one could argue that two women parent better on average than a woman and a man, or at least than a woman and man with a traditional division of family labor." This contention—that homosexual parenting is either neutral or better than traditional family structures—has found its way into our academic, legal, and cultural conversation and is rarely questioned. Hence the Ninth Circuit's declaration: "Children raised by gay or lesbian parents are as likely as children raised by heterosexual parents to be healthy, successful, and well-adjusted. The research supporting this conclusion is accepted beyond serious debate in the field of developmental psychology."

Regnerus's study was designed to reexamine this question—a difficult task, to say the least—by expanding the sample size and improving upon the methodology of previous surveys. The U.S. Census, for example, collects a lot of useful information but, because it does not ask questions about sexual orientation, much of its contribution to the topic must be inferred. Conversely, many academic studies that use the small-sample-size "snowball technique"—a process by which current subjects of a study recruit others from among their acquaintances to take part in it—can be misleading. One such study, discussed in Regnerus's paper, sampled women who frequented lesbian bookstores, events, and newspapers; the problem with this popular approach is

that it narrowed down the samples to the educated, probably afflu-
ent, and socially similar, and it produced a limited understanding as
a result. Such studies have proliferated in recent years.

In search of his answers, Regnerus screened 15,088 people. From
these, researchers found 175 people who had been raised for some of
their childhood by a mother who was in a lesbian relationship, and 73
people who had been raised for some of their childhood by a father
who was in a gay relationship—still a relatively small group.

The first thing that Regnerus found is that gay households with
children are located in the same geographical areas as the households
of straight couples raising kids. Contrary to stereotypes, there is no
real concentration of children where gays tend to live en masse. For
example, as there are few children in San Francisco's households overall, there are also few children living with gays in San Francisco. In
fact, Georgia is the state that has the most children living with same-
sex couples. Despite being allegedly less gay-friendly, Middle America
is very well represented in the gay-couple-with-child demographic.
And consistent with general trends, Latino gay couples have more
children than do white gay couples.

Demonstrators opposing gay marriage and gay adoption rally in France in April 2013.
Some studies have shown that children raised by same-sex couples underperform compared
with children raised by their biological parents.

Regnerus found that children in the study rarely spent their *entire* childhoods in the households of their gay parent and partner. Only two of the 175 subjects who reported having a mother in a lesbian relationship spent their whole childhood with the couple, and no children studied spent their entire childhood with two gay males. The numbers drop off pretty sharply as time progressed, too: For example, 57 percent of children spent more than four months with lesbian parents, but only 23 percent spent more than three years. This is interesting in and of itself, but it has serious implications for the study—implications to which I will later return.

Ultimately, Mark Regnerus set out to answer the question of whether children who have parents in a same-sex relationship experience disadvantages when compared with children raised by their biological, married parents. The answer, contra the zeitgeist, appears to be a resounding yes. Children with a parent in a same-sex relationship "underperform" in almost every category. Some of these differences may be relatively benign—whether one voted in the last presidential election, for example—but most are decidedly not. One deficit is particularly worrying: Less than 2 percent of children from intact, biological families reported experiencing sexual abuse of some nature, but that figure for children of same-sex couples is 23 percent. Similarly disturbing is that 14 percent of children from same-sex couples have spent some time in foster care, compared with around 2 percent of the American population at large. Arrest, drug experimentation, and unemployment rates were all higher among children from same-sex families.

What should we take away from this? Well, this is where it gets tricky. To compare children raised by same-sex parents with the "gold standard"—i.e., biological parents who remained married and alive— is problematic. Given the way the study is set up, one could fairly

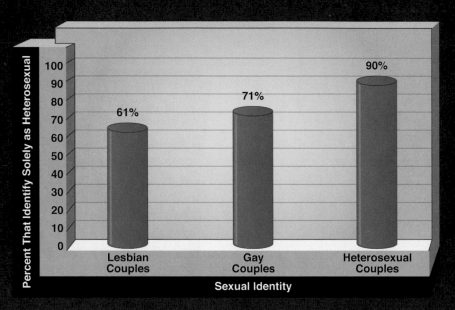

Sexual Self-Identity of Children of Same-Sex Couples Compared to Children of Heterosexual Couples

Taken from: Glenn T. Stanton. "Key Findings of Mark Regnerus' New Family Structure Study." *Focus on the Family*, June 2012. www.focusonthefamily.com/about_us/focus–findings/family–formation–trends/regnerus–family–structures–study.aspx.

ask whether this is not so much an analysis of homosexual parenting versus heterosexual parenting, but of childhood *stability versus instability*. By definition, any child raised by two members of the same sex is going to be missing at least one of their biological parents and will probably have experienced some instability in moving from the biological dyad to whatever arrangement replaced it. And, as explained above, most of the children studied spent only a few years with their same-sex parents, which makes it likely that their family arrangement changed more than once and, thus, that their childhood was unstable.

Moreover, given that the study is a snapshot of a time period that predated legalization of gay marriage (in some states), one might speculate that social stigma played a role in Regnerus's data, and that such stigma will have a smaller effect in future surveys. Indeed, one should concede that people could legitimately employ Regnerus's study to *justify* gay marriage on the grounds that societal disapproval of unmarried gay parents leads to the very instability that causes their children to experience negative outcomes: Marriage between gay partners will enhance the family's stability and therefore be good for the children. I consider this to be a step too far—the high rate of divorce among gays does not suggest that same-sex households will soon be a model of stability—but it is worth consideration.

Regnerus's study is a success insofar as it answers the fundamental question of whether children raised by same-sex couples end up differently: Clearly they do, and it does not require a conservative viewpoint to see that "differently" very often means "worse." It is debatable, though, whether this is an indictment of same-sex households or of instability. Indeed, the major takeaway from the report is less an indictment that same-sex households are a *negative* thing and more an affirmation that intact, biological households are a *positive* thing. Put simply, if you want to give your children the best start in life, you should have children inside of wedlock and stay together for the duration. But then, we already knew that.

EVALUATING THE AUTHOR'S ARGUMENTS:

How many different sources of information does Charles C.W. Cooke use to support his viewpoint? Compare his viewpoint to the previous viewpoint by Stephanie Pappas. Which viewpoint do you think is better supported, and why?

Viewpoint 3

Transracial Adoptions Should Be Encouraged

Ryan Bomberger

"We are a nation still so uncomfortable with the hue of our skin that we miss out on the ultimate act of racial reconciliation— loving a child of another race simply because they deserve to be loved."

In the following viewpoint Ryan Bomberger asserts that transracial adoptions should be encouraged. According to Bomberger, preserving a child's cultural identity is less important than finding the child a loving and permanent home. Having black children languish in foster care because there are not enough black families to adopt them is wrong, says Bomberger. He contends that racial politics need to be taken out of the adoption process. Bomberger is a journalist and blogger for LifeNews.com, an independent news agency devoted to reporting news that affects the pro-life community.

AS YOU READ, CONSIDER THE FOLLOWING QUESTIONS:

1. What does the Interethnic Placement Act prohibit, according to Bomberger?
2. According to researcher Rita Simon, as summarized in the viewpoint, what percentage of transracial adoptees agree with the National Association of Black Social Workers?
3. According to Bomberger, what does the biblical writing of James 1:27 charge us with doing?

Adoption is a powerful and emotionally potent act, for the birth mother and the prospective parents. The act of relinquishing a child to someone else and to take in a child, who is not biologically related, is an incredible act of love and sacrifice.

We need to foster an environment where people pursue adoption more and the public is educated about the beautiful stories that typify the adoption experience. This is part of the mission of The Radiance Foundation and its public awareness initiatives through TooManyAborted.com.

This August [2011] serves as the 15th year anniversary of significant action by Congress to help stop the racial politics affecting the placement of black foster children and recruitment of adoptive and foster parents. The Interethnic Placement Act, signed into law on August 20, 1996 by President [Bill] Clinton, barred any state or other entity that receives federal funds from using "race, color, or national origin of a child or of a prospective parent" in order to "make the child ineligible for foster care or adoption, or to deny a particular foster care or adoptive placement."

The author asserts that preserving a child's cultural identity is less important than finding the child a permanent, loving home.

The Racialization of Adoption

Tragically, this was to counter decades of the racialization of adoption where many child welfare groups placed culture above the most crucial needs of a foster child: to be loved and have a permanent home. In 1972, the National Association of Black Social Workers (NABSW), rooted in Black Nationalist ideology, declared:

> The National Association of Black Social Workers has taken a vehement stand against the placement of black children in white homes for any reason. We affirm the inviolable position of black children in black families where they belong physically, psychologically and culturally in order that they receive the total sense of themselves and develop a sound projection of their future.

FAST FACT

According to the Dave Thomas Foundation for Adoption's National Adoption Attitudes Survey from 2002, more than three-fourths of Americans say they would be very (40 percent) or somewhat (37 percent) likely to consider adopting a child who is of a different race.

So, is culture then preserved while the child awaits a family, languishing unnecessarily in foster care? Is ethnic identity more crucial than permanence?

Contrary to the claims of groups like NABSW and Child Welfare League, the preponderance of empirical studies prove that transracially adopted children are just as well adjusted as same-race adopted children. Researcher and esteemed scholar, Rita Simon, has conducted one of the most cited, in-depth longitudinal studies on the issue. Her research shows that 80% of transracial adoptees disagree with groups like the National Association of Black Social Workers. I'm one of those adoptees.

Black children remain in foster care at higher rates than other races and are disproportionately represented. There are a number of factors that influence this, but the main factor is race. We are a nation still so uncomfortable with the hue of our skin that we miss out on the ultimate act of racial reconciliation—loving a child of another race simply because they deserve to be loved. Same-race adoptions are beautiful as well as mixed-race adoptions.

Transracial Adoptions

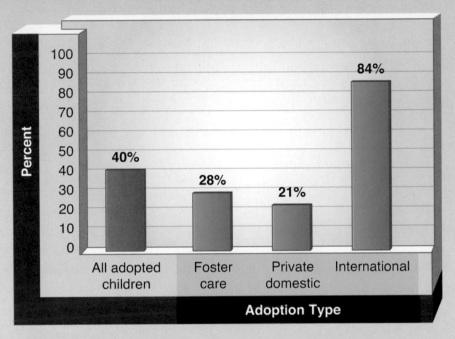

Percentage of adopted children who were adopted transracially in 2007, by adoption type

Taken from: US Department of Health and Human Services, *The National Survey of Adoptive Parents*, 2007.

For some reason, however, with every diatribe about racial healing and better cultural understanding, battle lines have been drawn around adoption. As long as we are human, the evil of racism will always exist. That should never stop us, however, from endeavoring to rid it where it harms the most vulnerable among us—the welfare of children. We are all guilty of our own prejudices, our firmly held stereotypes, our unwillingness to be proactive or more culturally competent (understanding others' cultures), and the inability to admit any of it.

The Need for Adoption

James 1:27 lays out a simple yet powerful framework for the purest form of religion: to take care of widows and orphans. To better understand this charge is to know the prevalence of war during those times that left countless women widowed and children orphaned, necessitating the call to conscience of those who believed in caring for those most vulnerable.

Today, although domestically we aren't ravaged by militaristic war, we are being decimated by a cultural war of abortion and abandonment that is leaving behind spouseless mothers and orphans, both born and unborn.

The Radiance Foundation and countless other life-affirming organizations, through community events, conferences and media campaigns, try to raise the level of awareness of the need for adoption and for more to be involved. Although the expectation isn't that every adult should or can adopt, we can all play a role fostering an environment that encourages adoption through our financial contributions, volunteering at pregnancy resource centers, supporting birth mothers and fighting material and spiritual poverty.

Laws like the Interethnic Placement Act are crucial but are not, necessarily, transformational of the heart and mind. Too often, needless racial politics mire adoption and foster care, to the detriment of the child, by those charged with their welfare. In the end, what children really need, regardless of race or ethnicity, is a place to call home and someone just to love them.

EVALUATING THE AUTHOR'S ARGUMENTS:

Do you think viewpoint author Ryan Bomberger's personal life experience makes his viewpoint stronger or weaker than if he had not been a product of transracial adoption? Explain.

Transracial Adoptions Should Not Be Encouraged

"These policies play into the popular misconception that colour blindness is a goal when in fact it is a disability."

Lemn Sissay

In the following viewpoint Lemn Sissay contends that adoption policies should be designed to place black children with black parents. According to Sissay, the British prime minister is changing Great Britain's adoption policies to make it easier for white parents to adopt black children, which Sissay believes is a mistake. Sissay believes that pretending race does not matter in adoption situations is a form of racism in itself. Sissay is a poet and playwright. He also writes for the *Guardian*, a British newspaper.

AS YOU READ, CONSIDER THE FOLLOWING QUESTIONS:

1. What was the uniting experience of the group of young adults that met on the fourth floor of the Children's Legal Centre in London in 1984, according to Sissay?
2. According to the author, what kind of fast-track adoptions occurred in the 1960s and 1970s?
3. As cited by Sissay, what two things would he not have done if he was "colour blind"?

"The most valuable resource of any ethnic group is its children. Nevertheless, black children are being taken from black families by the process of the law and being placed in white families. It is, in essence, 'internal colonialism' and a new form of the slave trade, but only black children are used."

These words were given in evidence to a House of Commons [lower house of Parliament in the United Kingdom] select committee, by the Association of Black Social Workers and Allied Professionals. Also in 1983, the social services committee report on children in care highlighted "the failure of the social services departments to recruit enough black foster and adoptive parents". Now David Cameron [prime minister of the United Kingdom] has decided to focus on making it easier for white couples to adopt black children. This shows how adoption policy is going backwards, ignoring decades of research-based practice.

Colour Blindness Is Not Always Good

These policies play into the popular misconception that colour blindness is a goal when in fact it is a disability. In this context, a disability is used to make those of colour and their needs invisible.

FAST FACT

Thirty-five percent of children who have been adopted from foster care, 25 percent adopted privately, and 3 percent adopted internationally are black, according to 2007 data from the US Department of Health and Human Services.

In 1984, a group of young adults met on the fourth floor of the Children's Legal Centre on Compton Terrace in Islington, north London. They had travelled from all over England and were united by one experience: they were black and either in care or had recently left care. It was difficult to talk, but then one spoke of bathing in bleach, another of being spat at and beaten and the floodgates opened. Another spoke of never knowing his own name. Another of her name being shortened or changed entirely to make it easier for those around her. Another spoke of being publicly stoned. The Black and In Care conference

British prime minister David Cameron speaks at a London children's center about his changing Great Britain's adoption policies to make it easier for white parents to adopt black children. The decision met with some opposition.

report and video—it was attended by 300 black people in care—were published in 1985. Partly as a result, the cause of same-race adoption and fostering was promoted by government and local authorities throughout the country as good practice.

Some 25 years of work by local authorities throughout Britain is being reversed in just two years of coalition government. And why? Cameron conflates the issue of speeding up adoption with the issue of same-race placements. Is this political sleight of hand?

Fast-track adoption has happened before. In the 1960s and 70s it relied on society's abhorrence and unwillingness to listen to the pregnant unmarried female. Women were removed from their community, isolated in mother and baby homes often run by nuns, and then coerced by social workers into signing adoption papers. Then the mothers were shipped back to their community, not to speak of

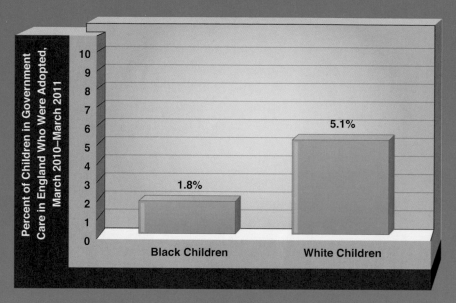

Percent of White Children Adopted from Government Care Is 2.8 Times Higher than for Black Children in England

Percent of Children in Government Care in England Who Were Adopted, March 2010–March 2011

10
9
8
7
6
5
4
3
2
1
0

5.1%

1.8%

Black Children

White Children

Taken from: UK Department for Education. "Children Looked After in England Year Ending 31 March 2011." www.education.gov.uk.

it. Those mother and baby homes were like child farms: the nuns the farmers, the social workers the landowners and prospective parents the consumers.

Gollywogs

Last week [March 2012], Abby Harrison, a mixed-race woman who has been in care, contacted me via Facebook. On Wigan [a town in northwestern England] market there were two gollywogs [rag dolls depicting a black character from nineteenth-century children's books] on two market stalls by two entrances. Abby, who has lived in Wigan all her life and has five mixed-race children, politely asked the stall-holder if he would mind removing them. He refused. It seems the users of Wigan market and the council owners don't mind. Cameron is setting out his adoption policy stall in the equivalent of Wigan market, where he knows the majority of consumers will not complain about the policy of fast-tracking black children to be adopted by white families because most of his customers are in fact white. And what's wrong with a gollywog anyway?

The point made in 1983 still stands: why has the government not put as much energy into finding black adopters? And besides, why say a family environment is all a child in care needs as quickly as possible when 50% of children in care have fled an abusive family environment as quickly as they could? And why say care is a bad thing—rather than "we can make it better"—if it is care under your watch?

The gollywogs are still hanging in Wigan market. If Abby convinced herself of colour blindness she wouldn't see them for the aggressive statement they are. If I were colour blind, I would never have written this article. And I wouldn't have been at that conference in 1984.

Seeing life in colour makes it more truthful, equal and naturally balanced, less black and white. I suggest Cameron does the same, otherwise in years to come another group of strangers will meet in a room and wait for someone else to speak first.

EVALUATING THE AUTHOR'S ARGUMENTS:

Ryan Bomberger, the author of the previous viewpoint, contends that placing a black child with a black family is less important than finding the child a loving and permanent home. What do you think is Lemn Sissay's main contention in his viewpoint? Do you think it is the opposite of Bomberger's contention? Explain.

Older-Parent Adoption Should Be Encouraged

Ann Brenoff

"It was as simple as this: We weren't finished being parents. We wanted to raise another child."'

In the following viewpoint Ann Brenoff asserts that people are never too old to become adoptive parents. Many older parents have already raised biological children but still have the desire to parent, says Brenoff. Others are first-time parents, fulfilling lifelong dreams and wanting to help a child, she says. Brenoff provides examples of parents who illustrate that they are not too old to adopt. Brenoff is a senior writer for the *Huffington Post,* an online news source.

AS YOU READ, CONSIDER THE FOLLOWING QUESTIONS:

1. At what age should people stop having children, according to respondents of a study on American attitudes toward aging and as cited in the viewpoint?
2. According to Brenoff, what changed Sandy Liaw's sixty-year-old husband's mind about adopting?
3. According to Brenoff, from what country did Judy Wolf adopt her daughter?

A recent study of Americans' attitudes toward aging contained this little gem: Respondents thought people should stop having children by age 41, on average. While nature—at least for women—may concur with the results, that hasn't stopped older couples from adopting when they are well into their 50s and even 60s, bucking the idea that they are too old to be parents.

Adam Pertman, executive director of the Evan B. Donaldson Adoption Institute and author of *Adoption Nation*, called [baby] boomers' [the large population born roughly between 1946 and 1964] embrace of adoption "a trend that's clearly happening," although he doesn't know of any group tracking the ages of adoptive parents. But, "without question, more of them are doing it," he said.

"The world has changed, but our biology hasn't," Pertman said. "Adoption fills that gap. People marry later, women are involved in the workplace—it makes even more sense to adopt. Women live well into their 80s. They can have a child when they are 50 and still live to see their grandkids. Older parents are very often happy—actually seek out—the adoption of an older child. This serves all parties and society."

You're never too old to adopt or love a child, say adoptive parents who were midlifers when they welcomed new family additions. In some cases, the parents had already raised children; for others, it was jumping on the parenting train for the first time before it left the station for good.

Wanting to Raise Another Child

When Judy and Don Criglow of Louisiana traveled to China 10 years ago to adopt then 2-year-old Abbie, they already had four grown children between them, ages ranging from 20 to 29. Judy was 50 and Don, 55, and their youngest was finishing college. "Our other children were grown, out-of-college, married adults when we went for Abbie," Judy said. "We actually had two grandchildren at the time—now there are three."

Judy said a lightbulb went off when she realized she was attempting to mother her two grandkids instead of "grandmothering" them: "It was simple as this: We weren't finished being parents. We wanted to raise another child," she said. "We just weren't the kind of people to buy an RV and go traveling."

The author argues that older adoptive parents are happier in their lives and that therefore they provide a more stable and loving home for adopted children.

The self-employed couple travels sometimes for work—they are in the Dallas [Texas] area for a six-month contract right now—and Abbie, who is home-schooled, travels with them. She is a good student, makes friends easily and is the apple of her parents' eyes.

While their adult kids "probably thought we were crazy when we first told them our plans to adopt," Judy said, they quickly came around. Now, it's like Abbie has three mommies, two of them her adult older sisters. Judy finds she is a more patient parent this time around: "You just don't sweat the small stuff. If she wants to eat her ice cream dessert before she sits down to dinner, it isn't the end of the world."

Fulfilling a Dream

When Sandy Liaw of Los Angeles adopted from China, she was fulfilling her lifelong dream of becoming a mom, just shy of her 50th birthday. When she brought home a beautiful little 13-month-old girl, her husband was 60. Sandy had battled infertility for years; her husband was initially uncomfortable with the idea of adoption until a [newswoman] Barbara Walters' special on her own adoption story convinced him otherwise.

"I always thought I should write Barbara Walters a letter, thanking her," Sandy said. "She changed my husband's mind, which in turn changed my life."

Although Sandy and her husband are now divorced, they share custody of their now 12-year-old daughter, Sofia. Sandy, a third-grade teacher, describes her life as "blissful and perfect." A few weeks ago, she dropped off her daughter at a birthday party and took a book to read under a tree in the park. "I just looked up at the sky and felt so very, very grateful," she said. "We are all healthy, doing well. A sense of calm and gratitude just came over me."

But surely parenting a pre-teen when you are 60 is just a wee bit harder? "I don't know because I never did it when I was younger, so I have nothing to compare it to," Sandy said. "But I think as a teacher, I come with a reserve of patience and energy." She and her daughter travel abroad together frequently; last summer, they went to China to attend a cultural camp.

> **FAST FACT**
>
> Over half (54 percent) of children adopted from the US foster care system have parents over age fifty, and 16 percent have parents over age sixty, according to data from the 2007 National Survey of Adoptive Parents and the 2007 National Survey of Children's Health.

Lori McCoy's adoption story had a more painful beginning: She lost her seven-month-old son to a form of muscular dystrophy. Her recovery from the death of her son took years. McCoy, who lives in the San Francisco Bay Area, was 47 when she and her husband adopted Chanti, a 3-1/2-year-old girl from Cambodia. That was 10 years ago.

At 57, Lori finds she's not the only older mom in her daughter's class. "I know many who are my age or darn near close to it. Honestly, my age isn't even a factor in our lives.

"I recently started a new job and am dead tired when I get home, but seeing my daughter always energizes me," McCoy continued. "I love hearing about her day and her life. My daughter is the best and most amazing part of my world. It's funny because I often find myself thinking about the whole nature vs. nurture argument. Chanti and I are so much alike with our personalities—and she was 3-1/2 when she came here, so there is a lot about her that I had nothing to do with. I'm the luckiest mom on Earth."

Karen Bradley, a 50-year-old single mom in the Phoenix area, had three biological children and then adopted another three. At the time of her last adoption, she was a week shy of her 46th birthday. "From a very early age, I always knew I wanted to adopt," she said. "I fostered kids for nine years, and after seeing children returned to homes that were less than ideal, I decided to pursue international adoption." Her first adoption was at age 40—Kevin, a 4-1/2-year-old boy from China. She then adopted two more times: Bryndan, a 2-1/2-year-old girl from China when she was 43 and a seven-month-old baby girl, Macyn, from Ethiopia when she was 45.

"In some ways, being an older parent is easier," Bradley said, "because I feel like I am more patient and have realistic expectations. I understood, and accepted the fact that adopting at such a late stage in my life would mean pushing retirement out until [Macyn] graduates college," Bradley said, adding, "[it's a] small price to pay for the absolute joy she brings to our lives."

Single adoptive mom Judy Wolf says that from day one, she's told her daughter that "our story is a love story between you, me and God." She describes herself as someone "born to be a mom."

Wanting to Change a Child's Life
"I never met Mr. Right and didn't want to pass up the opportunity to be a mom and change a child's life. So after several years of con-

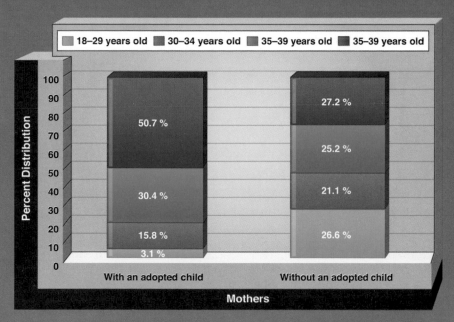

Adoptive Mothers Are Older than Mothers Who Have Not Adopted

Percent Distribution

Legend: 18–29 years old, 30–34 years old, 35–39 years old, 35–39 years old

With an adopted child:
- 50.7 %
- 30.4 %
- 15.8 %
- 3.1 %

Without an adopted child:
- 27.2 %
- 25.2 %
- 21.1 %
- 26.6 %

Mothers

Taken from: Jo Jones. "Who Adopts? Characteristics of Women and Men Who Have Adopted Children." *NCHS Data Brief*, January 2009.

sideration, at the ripe old age of 44, I made the decision to adopt my daughter," she said.

Her family, friends and the social worker who made the pre-placement visits questioned her choice. She heard things like "Children need both a mother and a father"; "Can you afford this?"; and "Most people your age are thinking about becoming a grand-parent, how will you respond to your peers?"

"The questions were crazy and endless," Judy said. "Although unprepared for all these questions, I handled them beautifully, because God was leading me. Nothing dissuaded me; I was eager to finally be a mom and provide love to my wonderful daughter."

In March of 2004, Wolf was shown a photo of a two-year-old in Belarus. She looked at the photo and knew instantly. "She was my daughter," Judy said. "I didn't care about her medical history, or anything else the adoption agency wanted to provide me. I just wanted to know when could I go get my daughter." Camryn Dorothy Wolf was named after family members who played a significant role in her mom's life. Her daughter is now 10 and Judy, 53.

How is it working out, being an older parent? "Gee, am I one?" she replied.

EVALUATING THE AUTHOR'S ARGUMENTS:

Ann Brenoff provides examples of older parents who are happy and providing stable and loving homes to their adoptive children. What impact would it have on her viewpoint if she provided examples of older adoptive parents who were not happy with their decision to adopt?

Viewpoint
6

Older-Parent Adoption Should Not Be Encouraged

"The answer is that a child will benefit from being adopted by younger parents."

Antonia Sage

In the following viewpoint Antonia Sage asserts that older people should not be encouraged to adopt. According to Sage, there are too many risks associated with older-parent adoption. She says older parents are more prone to stress, may face financial difficulties, and are likely to have difficulty connecting with their children. Children are better off with younger parents, says Sage. Sage is a member of Helium, an online community for writers.

AS YOU READ, CONSIDER THE FOLLOWING QUESTIONS:
1. According to Sage, why is civilized society obliged to examine the implications of adoption by those over age fifty?
2. As stated in the viewpoint, as we age, stress has a stronger impact on what?
3. According to the author, what are younger parents more likely to be in touch with because of generational proximity?

If [business magnates] Donald Trump and Rupert Murdoch can have children later in life, why not adoptive parents?

We live in an era that demands its own morality; traditional views of right and wrong neither appeal nor apply to degrees of social, political and ethical complexity we encounter. Advances in science and means have blurred traditional boundaries of family, gender and age. Want to change your gender? No problem. Want to have a child well after menopause? No problem. Want to marry someone thirty years younger? No problem.

Well, there is a problem. Choices have consequences.

Should adoption by those over age 50 be permitted? The consequences and risks of this choice are complex, because they also impact the adopted child. Because an orphaned child does not have a say in the decision of its adoption, because that decision alone can transform her life, a civilized society is obliged to examine the implications of this decision on her behalf.

It is true that an orphaned child will benefit from a home, even in the care of older parents. But we are not discussing absolutes here. Hopefully, the choice is not between leaving a child remain orphaned versus being adopted by older parents, but between being adopted by younger rather than older parents. In which case, the answer is that a child will benefit from being adopted by younger parents. Here is why:

Younger Adults Make Better Parents

The most important function of parenting is creating a nurturing environment for the child, which requires emotional readiness to put the interests of the child first. Although rewarding, raising a child is a highly stressful activity. Stress and aging are strongly interconnected.

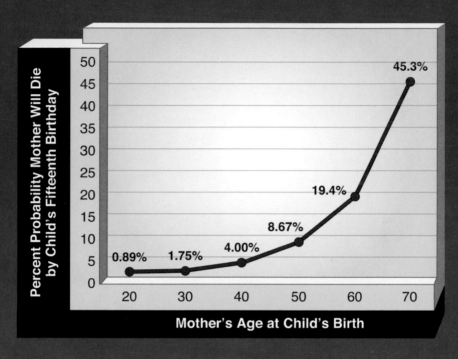

Children of Older Moms Are More Likely to Suffer Mom's Death by Fifteen Years Old

Percent Probability Mother Will Die by Child's Fifteenth Birthday

- 0.89%
- 1.75%
- 4.00%
- 8.67%
- 19.4%
- 45.3%

Mother's Age at Child's Birth

Taken from: Julianne Zweifel, Sharon Covington, and Linda Applegarth. "Last-Chance Kids": A Good Deal for Older Parents—but What About the Children?" *Sexuality, Reproduction, and Menopause (SRM)*, May 2012.

As we age, stress has a stronger impact on our physical and emotional wellbeing, compromising our immune and neurological systems, causing depression, a common response to stress among older adults.

Older parents are likely to be nearing retirement. Options to create income decline with age, and providing for the needs of a growing child, for her education, interests and future may present a greater challenge to older parents. Younger parents, on the other hand, have an advantage of time, and can work to overcome any financial disadvantage they may have, starting out. They are also likely to be financially independent when the children grow into adults, and in a position to help them out if need arises. Parents who adopt in their fifties will be in their seventies when their children reach adulthood—a time when financial demands of health and healthcare may outstrip means.

Opponents of adoption by older parents say older people are more susceptible to stress, may face financial difficulties, and are more likely to have difficulty relating to their children.

Younger parents are more likely to have a peer group of other parents, and more likely to create shared experiences children cherish, like play dates and sleepovers. Younger parents, because of generational proximity, are likelier to be in touch with the social environment children inhabit today, and be more accommodating and supportive. Older parents, with the best of intentions, may feel challenged to keep up with the child's interests, and may even fail to comprehend some of their experiences.

It is easier for younger parents to stay up nights tending to sick children, driving to the hospital at midnight and sitting awake through wee hours waiting for medical attention in case of an emergency. Older parents, on the other hand, are likely to experience declining health, with a corresponding drop in energy levels, which will compromise the extent to which they can act as successful caregivers. Advancing age may also shift the burden of care giving to the children very early.

It has been argued correctly that there are no guarantees to life. It is possible that older parents will live longer, and younger parents may die early, even after providing for the real time probabilities (which favor younger parents). However, regardless of the assumption we make about longevity, the risks are different. If, by a cruel quirk of fate, younger parents are taken away, the child may yet be raised by siblings (likely to be young), or grandparents. What happens when older parents die?

Older Parents' Desires Do Not Outweigh the Risks

"Because I want to" is not a good reason for a teenager, and it is not a good reason for an older adult while pursuing an action that may appear unconventional. Older adults may want to adopt for a multitude of reasons, ranging from the desire to help orphans, to experience parenthood because they found a suitable life partner later in life, or to just have a sense of family that comes from having a house with kids. All of these may be good reasons to seek to adopt, but they must be weighed against risks and alternatives, the importance being placed on the wellbeing of the child, which is the true hallmark of good parenting.

EVALUATING THE AUTHOR'S ARGUMENTS:

The author of the previous viewpoint, Ann Brenoff, asserts that older parents are happy and are making it work, while Antonia Sage, in this viewpoint, says children are better off with younger parents. Whose viewpoint do you agree with, and why? Do you think there are any points upon which both authors might agree? If so, what are they?

Chapter 3

What Policies Should Govern Adoption?

Open adoption, where the birth parents and adoptive parents both have a role in raising the child, is becoming more commonplace, but it is not without controversy.

Doing What's Best for the Tribe

Marcia Zug

"American Indian families and tribes are struggling to recover from the devastating history of forced removal, but such recovery is impossible if they continue to lose their children."

In the following viewpoint Marcia Zug argues that policies requiring the placement of adoptable Native American, or American Indian, children in American Indian homes are necessary. The US law establishing this policy is the Indian Child Welfare Act (ICWA). According to Zug, this law was enacted to protect Indian children and promote the stability of Indian families and tribes. The law is necessary, says Zug, because there was a long period in the United States in which American Indian children were removed from their families and tribes and placed with adoptive families who were not American Indian. Zug says the 2012 case in which a court ordered a two-year-old child to be removed from her adoptive home and reunited with her American Indian father is heart rending. But, says Zug, the court's decision was called for under the ICWA, and it was the right response. Zug is an associate law professor specializing in family and American Indian law at the University of South Carolina School of Law.

AS YOU READ, CONSIDER THE FOLLOWING QUESTIONS:
1. What year was the ICWA enacted, as stated in the viewpoint?
2. According to Zug, the US Supreme Court issued only one decision about the ICWA, and it occurred in 1989. What was the name of the court case that brought about the decision?
3. According to the author, the Capobiancos hope to reduce tribal control over American Indian child adoptions and revive what?

On July 26, the South Carolina Supreme Court issued a decision affirming the return of Veronica, an adopted 2-year-old Cherokee child, to her biological father, Dusten Brown. The court's decision was devastating for her adoptive parents, Melanie and Matt Capobianco, who had been raising the child since her birth after her biological mother willingly gave her up for adoption. "I'll always remember her crying when we had to—we had to walk out of that office and leave her there," said Melanie Capobianco referring to Veronica's reunification with Brown. "We're kind of reeling from it, and reliving having to hand her over in our minds constantly is painful," the couple added.

Since Veronica's reunification with Brown in January, the Capobiancos have been fighting ceaselessly for her return. Veronica's case has garnered national attention and unprecedented support. For months, pictures of the smiling toddler with her adoptive parents have been splashed across South Carolina papers and featured on CNN and in the *Weekly Standard*. Moreover, these news stories about "Baby Veronica" almost uniformly support the Capobiancos, with articles and commentary expressing outrage at the fact that although South Carolina law supports terminating Brown's parental rights due to his lack of involvement and financial support before and after Veronica's birth, this state law is superseded by an "obscure law" or "federal loophole" known as the Indian Child Welfare Act (ICWA).

ICWA is a federal statute that regulates the custody and placement of American Indian children. Brown is an enrolled member of the Cherokee tribe, and Veronica is also eligible for membership. As a result, ICWA applies to Veronica's adoption, supersedes state law, and mandates her reunification with Brown. Many Native American law scholars and advocates believe that ICWA is the most important American Indian law ever enacted, but its application in this case has caused fury. More than 20,000 people have signed the "Save Veronica" petition, which calls for an amendment to ICWA to prevent the return of children like Veronica. However, ICWA is no "loophole." The act specifically contemplated situations like Veronica's, and in this case, ICWA operated exactly as it was intended to.

ICWA was enacted in 1978 "to protect the best interests of Indian children and to promote the stability and security of Indian tribes and families." It was also a federal recognition of the long history of forced removal of American Indian children from their families and tribes by nontribal public and private agencies. Beginning in 1869, the United States removed thousands of American Indian children from their families and tribes and sent them to government board-ing schools. In these schools, American Indian children were given European names, forbidden to speak their own language, barred from practicing their religion or culture, and prevented from seeing their

Dusten and Robin Brown of the Cherokee Nation prepare a meal at home for their daughter Veronica. The Browns won custody of Veronica from her adoptive parents when a federal court upheld a federal law that prohibits the adoption of Native American children outside their tribe.

families. Hundreds (some say thousands) of American Indian children never returned and were lost to their families and tribes. Eventually, the boarding schools were shut down, but they were replaced with an equally devastating policy of nonnative adoption. Between 1958 and 1967, the Indian Adoption Act was used to remove hundreds of Native American children from their homes and place them with adoptive families who were not American Indians. The purpose of these policies was assimilation—the extinction of the tribes as separate entities.

Although it has been decades since these policies of forced assimilation ended, the effects continue to be felt. A century of removing American Indian children wreaked havoc on Native American families and tribes. Even after the passage of ICWA, the percentage of American Indian children in foster care and placed for adoption remains astonishingly high. American Indian families and tribes are struggling to recover from the devastating history of forced removal, but such recovery is impossible if they continue to lose their children. Congress recognized this struggle and intentionally drafted ICWA to cover both the involuntary removal of American Indian children from American Indian families and the voluntary placement of American Indian children outside of American Indian families.

Congress understood that in order to ensure a tribe's control over its children and its future, ICWA must also apply to voluntary placements.

Under ICWA, Veronica is a Native American child, and her Native American heritage was neither a secret nor a surprise. Everyone involved in Veronica's adoption was aware she was American Indian and that this could complicate the adoption, even though it was voluntary. The U.S. Supreme Court affirmed this understanding of ICWA in 1989 in *Mississippi Band of Choctaw v. Holyfield*, its first and only ICWA decision. *Holyfield* involved a pregnant Choctaw mother who wished to place her unborn twins with a non–Native American couple. Although the mother lived on the Choctaw reservation, she specifically left the reservation to give birth in the hope that this move would make ICWA inapplicable to her children's adoption. Despite the mother's significant efforts to avoid tribal jurisdiction and control her children's adoptive placement, the court held that the placement decision remained the tribe's. The decision further explained that the tribe's right to its children and an American Indian child's right to grow up American Indian outweighed individual tribal members' rights to place their children for adoption outside the tribe. The court understood that permitting voluntary adoptions to bypass ICWA's requirements could defeat the entire purpose of the act.

As the *Holyfield* decision made clear, even in voluntary placements, the child's tribe must be notified and ICWA's placement preferences followed. Thus, when an American Indian child is available for adoption, preference is first given to a member of the child's extended family, second to other members of the child's tribe, and third to other Native American families. Only after such placement preferences have been exhausted may nonnative adoption be considered. This process did not happen in Veronica's case, so her adoption was a clear violation of ICWA. It should never have happened, but the situation is heart-wrenching because despite the inappropriateness of her adoption, placement did occur and lasted for two years. Nonetheless, if the passage of time were enough to defeat ICWA, then the requirements of the act could simply be avoided by delay and obfuscation.

The Capobiancos are now hoping to petition the U.S. Supreme Court and Congress to amend ICWA, and as parents, their actions are understandable. However, the remedy they seek would be disastrous for American Indian tribes. Through congressional amendment or Supreme Court decision, the Capobiancos hope to reduce tribal control over American Indian child adoptions and revive the "existing Indian family exception" to ICWA. This doctrine is a judicially created exception that courts have used to avoid the application of ICWA in cases where the court determines the child is not part of a sufficiently American Indian family. The idea behind the exception is that in cases involving American Indian children who have never been part of an American Indian home, such as children placed for adoption at birth, ICWA should not apply because there is no

Disproportionate Numbers of American Indian and Alaska Native Children Are in State Foster Care

State	Percent of State's Child Population Who Are American Indian and Alaska Native	Percent of Foster Care Children Who Are American Indian and Alaska Native
Alaska	20	50.9
Minnesota	2	12.2
Montana	10	33.6
Nebraska	1	9
North Dakota	9	26.2
Oregon	1	11.3
South Dakota	15	52.2
Utah	1	5.7
Washington	2	8.4

Taken from: Terry Cross. "A 'Mission Not Impossible.'" *National Indian Child Welfare Association*, 2011; National Indian Child Welfare Association and The Pew Charitable Trusts. *Time for Reform: A Matter of Justice for American Indian and Alaskan Children*, 2007.

"Indian family" being destroyed by the adoption. The problem with this exception is that it ignores the fact that ICWA was passed not simply to preserve specific American Indian families but to protect the tribe's interest in the adoption of American Indian children as well. As the court held in *Holyfield*, ICWA is "a means of protecting not only individual Indian children and their families, but also of the tribes themselves." Although this exception, first introduced in 1982, was initially embraced by many states, the doctrine has now been almost universally rejected. Courts rejecting the exception understand that without ICWA, the future of American Indian tribes is imperiled.

Veronica's case is deeply troubling, and our hearts should go out to all involved, but the problems it highlights are not problems with ICWA. Rather, her case reveals the problems with ignoring ICWA. This case agonizingly demonstrates the importance of observing

ICWA's placement and termination procedures in order to prevent impermissible adoptions from occurring and then being invalidated later. Everyone involved in Veronica's adoption knew she was an American Indian child, and if the ICWA requirements had been followed, Veronica would not have been placed with the Capobiancos in the first place. It was because of this mistake that Veronica was 2 years old rather than an infant when she was reunited with her father. The lesson from Veronica's case is not that ICWA is some obscure loophole that should be closed. Rather, the ongoing court battle demonstrates that ICWA is a pivotal piece of American Indian legislation that cannot be ignored without traumatic consequences

EVALUATING THE AUTHOR'S ARGUMENTS:

Do you think Marcia Zug has made a strong argument in support of the Indian Child Welfare Act? Why or why not? How could the circumstances of Baby Veronica's case, in which a two-year-old had to be taken away from the only parents she knew, have been avoided, according to Zug?

Viewpoint

2

Policies Mandating the Placement of American Indian Children in American Indian Homes Are Harmful

"The idea that a nearly 3-year-old child's alleged ethnic heritage trumps her right to remain with loving parents in the only home she has ever known is reason for pause."

Ethan Epstein

In the following viewpoint Ethan Epstein maintains that the Indian Child Welfare Act (ICWA), which attempts to keep Native American, or American Indian, children with American Indian families, is harmful. Epstein discusses the Baby Veronica case, in which the ICWA required that a toddler be taken away from her adoptive parents and placed with her father, who is part Cherokee. Epstein says there may have been good reasons to enact the ICWA in 1978. However, it has become a harmful law that is tearing families apart. Epstein is an editorial assistant at the conservative newsmagazine the *Weekly Standard*.

AS YOU READ, CONSIDER THE FOLLOWING QUESTIONS:
1. What percentage Cherokee is Baby Veronica's father, according to Epstein?
2. According to the author, some advocates of the ICWA say that "Indian children don't experience attachment like non-Indians do." As explained by these advocates, who or what are Indian children more likely to attach to?
3. How many attorneys does Epstein say the Cherokees are employing to target fifteen hundred children nationwide for removal?

In 1978, a little-known law called the Indian Child Welfare Act was signed with the intention of keeping families together. Today, it's being used to tear them apart.

Take the case of the Capobianco family of James Island, South Carolina. Matt Capobianco, who works at Boeing, and his wife Melanie, a psychologist, spent years trying to conceive a child, even going so far as to attempt in-vitro fertilization seven times. The couple ultimately decided to adopt, and found a pregnant mother in Oklahoma who was willing to give them her child. So taken with the Capobiancos was the birth mother that she even let Matt cut the umbilical cord when the little girl, whom the Capobiancos named Veronica, was born in September 2009. The child's birth father waived his parental rights, declaring that he "would not be responsible in any way for child support or anything else as far as the child's concerned," and Matt and Melanie took Veronica back to South Carolina, where they began to raise her as their own.

Four months later, Veronica's birth father, a soldier in the U.S. Army living in Oklahoma named Dusten Brown, changed his mind and initiated legal proceedings to gain custody of Veronica. Normally, this would have been an easy win for the Capobiancos; not only had Brown signed away his rights, he had also provided no support through the pregnancy. But there was a hitch.

A Drop of Indian Blood
The Indian Child Welfare Act [ICWA] ensures that in custody cases involving adoptions and foster care, preference is always given to

Survey results from sixteen state child welfare agencies reporting how many children remain in foster care longer than otherwise as a result of following ICWA procedures, fiscal year 2003

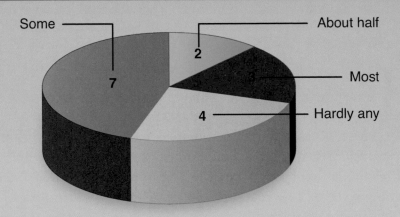

Some

About half

2

7

Most

3

4

Hardly any

Taken from: US Government Accountability Office. "Indian Child Welfare Act," April 2005.

keeping Indian children in Indian families. Using this law, Brown—who is reportedly 3 percent Cherokee, . . . enlisted the Cherokee tribal council to help him sue for custody. Because Veronica has "a drop of Cherokee blood," she qualifies for tribal membership and thus is an "Indian child" under the Indian Child Welfare Act.

The Indian preference rule doomed the Capobiancos. After a two-year battle in family court, Veronica was removed from her home on December 31, 2011, and sent to Oklahoma to live with her biological father. "I'll always remember her crying when we had to walk out of that office and leave her there," Melanie told Charleston media. The family appealed the decision, but late last month, they lost in the South Carolina supreme court. The majority affirmed the family court's order under the Indian Child Welfare Act, though the justices noted that they did so "with a heavy heart."

The ICWA Puts Tribes' Rights Over Families' Rights

To be sure, the Indian Child Welfare Act was ratified, as the law itself states, at a time when "an alarmingly high percentage of Indian families [were] broken up by the removal of their children"—some estimates say that up to 35 percent of Indian children were being removed from their families at the time, ostensibly for reasons of abuse or parental incompetence. But the idea that a nearly 3-year-old child's alleged ethnic heritage trumps her right to remain with loving parents in the only home she has ever known is reason for pause. And some of the arguments made in support of the law are positively bizarre.

Its advocates claim, for example, that "Indian children don't experience 'attachment' like non-Indian children do because they are more likely to attach to the tribe rather than the primary caretakers." Thus, the law elevates the supposed rights of the group over the best interests of individual children. As Maurice Portley, an appellate judge in Arizona who has studied the law, explains, "the act revolutionized the 'best interests of the children' concept for Indian children. Instead of merely looking at the Indian child's stability in a placement and bond with a psychological parent, the federal standard requires an examination of 'the rights of the Indian child as an Indian and the rights of the Indian community and tribe in retaining [its] children in its society.'"

FAST FACT

According to the US Census Bureau, there were 557,425 American Indian and Alaska Native family households in 2011, and of these, 56.6 percent were married-couple families, including those with children.

Many Families Have Been Torn Apart

The Capobiancos are hardly the only family to have been torn apart as a result of this law. While there is no definitive national tally (foster care and adoption proceedings are generally kept private), Lisa Morris of the Christian Alliance for Indian Child Welfare, an organization that advocates for children hurt by the law, says

Melanie and Matt Capobianco talk to reporters about custody case involving the adoption of Baby Veronica.

that families contact her group seeking assistance fighting it "all the time." Morris also says that the Cherokee Nation, in particular, has been aggressive about marshaling the act to snatch children from their adoptive parents. She says the Cherokees have more than 100 attorneys targeting 1,500 children nationwide for removal from their families. The Cherokee Nation may be facing some headwinds, though: Another nonprofit, the Coalition for the Protection of Indian Children and Families, is lobbying Congress to amend the law to shorten the window during which an Indian biological parent can revoke his or her consent to an adoption.

EVALUATING THE AUTHOR'S ARGUMENTS:

Authors can reveal or promote their viewpoint by the words they use to convey information. For instance, in Ethan Epstein's viewpoint, he says the Cherokee Nation has been "aggressive" about using the Indian Child Welfare Act to "snatch" children from their adoptive parents. How do you think Marcia Zug, author of the previous viewpoint, might phrase this activity, and what words might she choose that are different than Epstein's? Can you identify any other places where Epstein's word choice reveals or promotes his viewpoint?

Open Adoption Is a Good Policy

Ian Stewart and Kathleen Silber

"Open adoption leads to better mental health in the children, birthparents and adoptive parents, and it has a higher success rate than closed."

Ian Stewart is a writer for the Independent Adoption Center, and Kathleen Silber is the center's associate executive director. She is also the author of *Dear Birthmother* and *Children of Open Adoption*. In the following viewpoint Stewart interviews Silber about the benefits of open adoption compared to closed adoption. The interview focuses on Silber's reaction to a morning show segment that Silber believes provided misinformation about open adoptions. According to Silber, the segment perpetuated the false notion that open adoptions are scary because birth mothers are horrible people that adoptive parents would not want to have in their lives. Knowledge and experience have dispelled this notion, says Silber. Open adoptions are more common and more successful than closed adoptions, she says.

AS YOU READ, CONSIDER THE FOLLOWING QUESTIONS:
1. Where does Silber say a lot of the misconceptions about closed adoption come from?
2. According to Silber, closed adoptions used to be the only choice. In what decade did she and others start noticing a lot more adult adoptees wondering about their past?
3. How many infant adoptions are open, according to Silber?

On June 8th [2012] NBC's *Today Show* ran a segment called "Today's Professionals Answer Viewer Questions." A panel of three "experts"—Donny Deutsch, a former advertising executive, Star Jones, an attorney, and Nancy Snyderman, a physician—answered audience questions on several subjects. A question was asked about the benefits of open vs. closed adoption and if the panelists had a preference. There was surprisingly no debate amongst the panel as all three said they were in favor of closed adoptions.

At IAC [Independent Adoption Center], we were surprised to see that a morning show with such a wide reach and mass audience would comment on the open vs. closed adoption topic without mentioning a single benefit of open adoption. We decided to take the opportunity to ask one of our nationally regarded experts, Independent Adoption Center Associate Executive Director Kathleen Silber, . . . to weigh in on how she felt about the segment and the benefits of open adoption compared to closed.

IAC: What was your initial reaction to the segment?

[Kathleen Silber]: Well honestly, it feels like a step back into dark ages, where closed adoption was still the norm. A lot has changed in adoption over the years. It's generally accepted knowledge now that an open adoption arrangement is not only healthier for the adoptees, but for the families as well. What's shocking about the commentary on the *Today Show* is actually how archaic those views are—it's hard to believe people are still advocating something that's known to not be good practice.

Misconceptions Based on Fear

What was your reaction to Nancy Snyderman saying that finding your birthmother is like "opening Pandora's box?"

That's a typical reaction of parents with a closed adoption and it's based out of a lot of fear. They don't know the birthmother or anything about her. What was sad about what was said on the show is that it just fed into the old stigmas about adoption that birthmothers are somebody horrible that you wouldn't want to have in your life. Birthmothers of open adoption know this is going to be a permanent long-term relationship where she knows her role is just the birthmother, not the parent. There is no mystery with open adoption because everything is out in the open.

Where do you think these misconceptions come from?

I think a lot of the misconceptions come from a lack of knowledge. It's a typical reaction for adoptive, or potential adoptive, parents to react based out of fear when they first hear and think about open adoption. A lot of times it's the initial reaction of "I just want to parent this baby. I don't want to have any contact with the birthmother because it sounds scary. I just want to adopt the baby, not the birthmother, too." And that stems from ignorance, because people think that the women who choose adoption for their babies are horrible people or have a bad history, but that's not the case.

Now when people go through the educational process about adoption they learn about the issues, particularly for children. It moves them past their needs and on to what the child's needs are going to be. It seems these supposed "experts" that responded were reacting out of what they felt were the parent's needs and not thinking about what the child's needs may be.

> ## FAST FACT
>
> According to a 2008 survey of one hundred private US adoption agencies by the Adoption Institute, 55 percent of adoptions were open, 40 percent were mediated, and 5 percent were closed.

If you were on the panel, how would you have responded?

You know, closed adoption used to be the only choice, but back in the early 1980's we started noticing a lot more of the adult adoptees were wondering about their past and they had so many unanswered questions it was hard for them to cope. We've learned through research and working with these families and children that open adoption leads to better mental health in the children, birthparents and adoptive parents, and

US Attitudes About Open Adoption

Question: "Do you think this is a good idea in most cases, in some cases, in very few cases, or in no cases at all?"

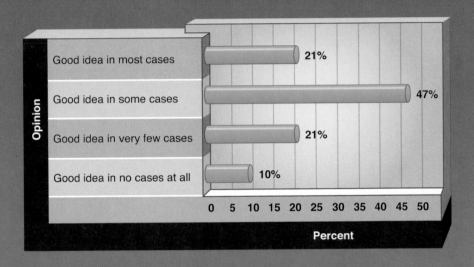

Question: "Do you think this is a good idea because . . . ?"

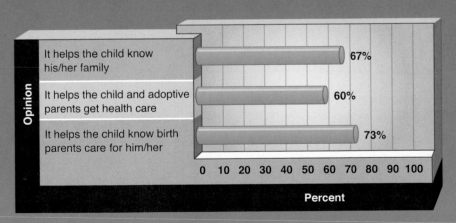

Base: All respondents (1,416 for open adoption a good idea; and 1,244 for why it is a good idea).

Taken from: Dave Thomas Foundation for Adoption. National Adoption Attitudes Survey, June 2002.

Due to an open adoption law, Maura Duffey (shown), who was adopted at birth, was able to find her birth mother and is thankful for the support she received from both her adoptive parents and birth mother.

it has a higher success rate than closed because of this. It doesn't matter how great a child's adoptive parents are at raising them, a child wants to know where they came from. Children who grow up obsessing over unanswered questions tend to develop problems. It's hard to grow up not knowing "Who do I look like?" and "Why was I given up?" Some children do alright with it, but others develop serious psychological problems. Comparatively, with open adoption, a child knows the answers to all these questions. They grow up so much better from a mental health point of view.

Extra Love Can Only Help, Not Hurt

How does contact with the birthparents work in open adoption?

I think when people first hear about open adoption they think, "Oh this is going to be confusing to the child, they're not going to know who their mom is," well, kids are smarter than that. They figure out who mom is because that's the person that's there everyday. So say if the birthmother were to come visit or something and the child falls down and skins his knee, who is the child going to run to? He's not going to run to the birthmother, he's going to run to his mom, the one who's been raising him.

It's best to view birthparents as extended family members who visit the child maybe once or twice a year. While there's a place in the child's life for these family members, there's no confusion about who "Mom" and "Dad" are. After all, your child cannot have too many people in his life who love him, and a little extra love will only help your child build a more positive self-concept.

These days, what percentage of adoptions are open compared to closed?

At this point a minimum of 80% of all infant adoptions are open. That's the national average and I believe it's even higher than that. That's why it seems irresponsible to advocate closed adoption on national television.

Contrary to popular opinion, closed adoption is actually much more prone to failure than open. Even if someone is interested in a closed adoption it's hard to find an agency for it these days. And modern tools like social media make closed adoption a thing of the past. Pretty soon, there will be no distinction between open and closed adoption—it will only be open.

> ## EVALUATING THE AUTHOR'S ARGUMENTS:
>
> Do you think Kathleen Silber's viewpoint is more focused on conveying the benefits of open adoption, or do you think it is more focused on defending open adoption against its detractors? Which approach do you think makes a more convincing argument?

Open Adoption Can Be Difficult

Amy Seek

> *"Open adoption is an awkward choreography; I am offered a place at the table, but I am not sure where to sit."*

In the following viewpoint Amy Seek shares her story of open adoption and asserts that such adoptions are not always easy. She reveals the pain of giving her son, Ben, up for adoption. It is a pain that endures, particularly as she watches him grow and realizes what she gave up. However, Seek is comforted by seeing Ben with his adoptive family, and she understands that openness is difficult for adoptive parents as well. According to Seek, open adoptions only work if adoptive parents are committed to maintaining a relationship with the birth mother and nurturing the birth mother–child relationship. Holly, the woman who adopted Seek's son, exemplifies this commitment, Seek asserts. Seek is a landscape architect who works on community food projects in New York City.

1. Seek describes adoption as balancing the equation. What are the two parts of the equation that become whole again, according to Seek?
2. What was one of the exercises Seek was given in adoption counseling?
3. What did Seek realize when she was able to say aloud that she wanted her son back, even though she knew it was impossible?

I wanted my son to become the kind of person who appreciates the beauty of the world around him, so I smiled when, at 6, he asked to borrow my camera in case he saw "something beautiful."

We were taking a walk in the woods outside Boston, and following behind him I was surprised by how much he moved like his father. We spent that afternoon showing each other icicles and hollow trees, breaking frozen patterns in the river ice, inching too close to the water to get a better view of the bridge above.

When we arrived home, Ben said that the reason he wanted to go for a walk was to spend time with me. It had been three months since I last saw him. I smiled sheepishly and stepped into the living room, where the woman who had adopted him six years earlier sat reading the newspaper.

I spent the evening chatting with her while avoiding direct interaction with Ben for fear I'd show too much affection, or too little. Open adoption is an awkward choreography; I am offered a place at the table, but I am not sure where to sit. I don't know how to be any kind of mother, much less one who surrendered her child but is back to help build a Lego castle.

Balancing the Equation

It is a far cry from the moment he was born, when my 23-year-old body seemed to know exactly what to do, when I suddenly and surprisingly wanted nothing more than to admire him nursing at my breast. When, after a drugless labor, my surging hormones helped me to forget that I was a college student, that I lived in Cincinnati, that I was passionate about architecture. During those days I was roused by the slightest sound of his lips smacking, innocent newborn desire that offered my deepest fulfillment.

In the months before I gave birth, when my boyfriend and I were just getting to know the couple we had chosen, I was able to comprehend the coming exchange only on the most theoretical of levels, but it seemed like gentle math: Girl with child she can't keep plus woman who wants but can't have child; balance the equation, and both parties become whole again.

During those months, my son's mother, Holly, observed that birth mothers have to accomplish in one day the monumental task of letting go that most parents have 18 years to figure out. Days after his birth, when I struggled with letting go, Holly sat with me and cried—for the children she never got to have, for the fact the adoption would bring her joy while causing me pain, and out of fear that she had already grown to love a child I might not give her.

I decided to let her take him for a night, to see if I could handle it. She drove him to Dayton, Ohio, where she was staying with family, then called and asked: "Do you want him back? I'll bring him right now."

Meanwhile, the men in our lives stood by and hoped for the best. My boyfriend supported the adoption, and though we had broken up, he was there to help me through my pregnancy. We had met in architecture school, never suspecting that two years later we would be forever joined as birth parents, composing 111 questions to ask strangers about the most intimate details of their lives.

We had a list of qualities we wanted in a couple—basically ourselves, 10 years older. But when we met the couple we would choose, our list fell by the wayside, replaced by an overwhelming intuition that we could trust them.

Sketching My Life Without My Son

I signed the papers on a hot August day in 2000, sitting at a large conference table with my sister, my son's adoptive parents and agents from Catholic Social Services. I'd sat there several times before but hadn't yet been able to say the words to relinquish all rights to my son. Each time I was left alone to think and, hours later, was sent home with him.

Cons of Open and Closed Adoptions

Party Involved	Closed Adoptions	Open Adoptions
Birth Parents	• Less grief resolution due to lack of information about the child's well-being. • May encourage denial of fact that child was born and placed with another family.	• Full responsibility for setting relationship limits and boundaries. • Potential abuse of trust (fewer safeguards). • Potential disappointment if adoptive family cannot meet all expectations or needs. • Birth mother may feel obligated to place child due to the emotional or financial support given by the prospective adoptive parents.
Adoptive Parents	• Allows for denial of "adopted family" or fertility status. • Increased fear, less empathy for birth parents. • No access to additional medical information about birth family. • Less control: Agency controls information.	• Full responsibility for setting relationship limits and boundaries. • Potential pressure: accept openness or no child. • Potential difficulty with emotionally disturbed birth parents. • Potential for supporting both child and birth parents (emotionally).
Adopted Persons	• Possible adolescent identity confusion (unable to compare physical and emotional traits to their birth families). • Limited access to information that others take for granted. • Potential preoccupation with adoption issues.	• No clean break for assimilation into family, which some feel is necessary. • Potential feelings of rejection if contact stops. • Difficulty explaining the the relationship to peers. • Potential for playing families against each other.

Taken from: Child Welfare Information Gateway. "Openness in Adoption," 2003.

My ex was not there; the birth had made me a different person, and we couldn't pretend that our losses would be the same. My sister had come from China, where she was teaching; she promised that if I kept him, she would move home and help. Her face was glazed in tears, but she stared intently at me as I prepared to sign the papers, as if to assure herself I knew what I was doing.

My pen rested at the intersection of two vastly different futures, and I struggled to see into the distance of each. It did not seem that a gesture as small as scribbling my name had the power to set me down one path while turning the other, its entire landscape, to dust. It was such a small gesture, but it was the first sketch of my life without a son.

One of the exercises I was given in adoption counseling was to envision the hours immediately after the adoption. What would I do after signing the papers? Pick up the towels that had been tossed in the corner when my water broke? Pack up the extra blankets I'd been given by the hospital workers who touched my shoulder and prayed aloud that I would find the courage to keep my son?

I had spent my entire life without a child, but I was newly born that night, too, and my old self disappeared. I could no longer imagine how a mother could give up a child and live. Adoption was not simple math; a new mother cannot know the value of the thing she subtracts. It is only through time—when my son turned 4, and I was 27; when he turned 6, and I was 29; when he turns 10 this year, and I am 33, and ready for children—that I begin to understand the magnitude of what I lost, and that it is growing.

My Son and His Family

The comfort is seeing my son with his family, whom I can no longer imagine him or myself without. He is an earnest child who seems

Kit Young (left), birth mother of Katie (far right), spends time with Katie and the child's adoptive mother, Laurie Sanders. The viewpoint author argues that such relationships can be difficult.

to kick hard to keep his chin above water in the world, but his mother has a certain lack of sympathy that is good for him. When he wants to retreat into his own head, she pulls him back into the refuge of his family and makes him smile. I am ever astounded that I was able to see in her something that would still feel so right so many years later.

The greatest proof of her commitment to openness is that she talks about me when I'm not there. When my son was a baby, I was surprised that he always remembered me, even after long stretches when I couldn't visit. When he was 7 and we were playing a computer game, he told me his password was "Cincinnati" because his mother had told him he was born there. I know that Holly represents me to my son in my absence and always encourages him to love me.

Holly jokes that with open adoption, at least you know what the birth mother is doing, that she's busy at school and not conceiving a plot to steal her child back. It's not so with closed adoptions; the birth mother is powerfully absent. But an open process forces an adoptive parent to confront the pain that adoption is built on. And openness for Holly does not mean merely letting the birth mother know about her child; it means cultivating a real love between birth parents and child. This requires exceptional commitment, which may be why some open adoptions become closed in the end.

I love Holly for sharing such things with me, sentiments that show she is devoted to our relationship—and not because it is easy for her. And I have told her that a pivotal point in my grief was the moment I was able to say aloud that I wanted my son back, though I knew it was impossible—when I realized that his adoption had been both my greatest accomplishment and deepest regret.

Preserving What We Cannot Keep

And we continually redefine this relationship. I hide certain exchanges, like the time he was 4 and crawled into my arms and said, "Amy, pretend I'm your baby."

I made sure no one was looking before I indulged his request, my entire body shuddering at the chance to hold him so close for the first time since birth. I suspect Holly knows about these moments, and when I visit she tries to help by sending me off with my son for walks in the woods, where we can freely explore my place in his life.

When I returned home to New York after my visit, I looked at the pictures Ben had taken with my camera: fragments of arms and legs, blurry close-ups of leaves caught in ice, too many spinning forest skies. Evidence to me that although he has his father's distinctive gait, he shares my need to grasp and hold on to beautiful things, to document and to somehow preserve them forever—things he can't possibly keep.

EVALUATING THE AUTHOR'S ARGUMENTS:

Amy Seek's viewpoint is a first-person account of open adoption. If you were interviewing Seek for a story on the pros and cons of open adoption versus closed adoption, what questions would you ask her, and why?

Laws Are Needed to Open Adoption Records

David Phelps and Joyce Bahr

"Why in the twenty first century are there laws nullifying a person's right to know the basic facts of their birth?"

In the following viewpoint David Phelps and Joyce Bahr urge state legislators to enact laws opening up birth records to all adoptive persons. According to Phelps and Bahr, most of the state laws that keep adoption records sealed were enacted years ago and were based on the myth that birth mothers wanted confidentiality. Sealed records laws are antiquated and discriminatory, depriving adopted persons of the fundamental human need to know where they come from, the authors say. Phelps and Bahr are members of the Unsealed Adoption Initiative, which seeks to open adoption records in the state of New York. Phelps was given up for adoption in 1960; Bahr relinquished her child for adoption in 1966.

AS YOU READ, CONSIDER THE FOLLOWING QUESTIONS:
1. When did the United Kingdom open its adoption records, according to Phelps and Bahr?
2. According to the authors, a study by Elizabeth Samuels concluded that laws closing records were not enacted as a shield to protect birth mothers, but as what?
3. What organization conducted the 2007 study that Phelps and Bahr say concluded that adoptees behave with maturity and respect when contacting members of their natural families?

Members of New York's "Unsealed Initiative," having ended a legislative lobby session in Albany for the Bill of Adoptee Rights, are in solidarity with protesters at the National Conference of State Legislatures annual conference in Chicago, Illinois in August 2012. Exasperated with outdated laws dating back to the 1930's which sealed original birth certificates forever, advocates for change and reform in adoption want legislators to know they will no longer tolerate unfairness, discrimination and disrespect. Why in the twenty first century are there laws nullifying a person's right to know the basic facts of their birth?

The United Kingdom opened adoption records more than three decades ago in 1975. Some countries throughout the world never sealed their adoption records and others that did have changed their laws since the 1980's, providing adopted people their long overdue rights. American adult adoptees have also had some success in changing antiquated adoption legislation. Recent legislation in Alabama, Maine, New Hampshire, Oregon and Rhode Island has restored legal recognition of their full human dignity.

> **FAST FACT**
>
> According to the Green Ribbon Campaign for Open Records, as of March 2013 seven states offered open or semi-open adoption records: Alabama, Alaska, Delaware, Kansas, Maine, Oregon, and Tennessee.

Myths and Unproven Fears

Archaic and false adoption myths, the adoption industry, some adoptive parent legislators and legislators fearing that opening records will necessarily lead to an increase in abortion have all conspired to impede legislative progress in the U.S. Adopted persons have been made to feel shame and fear simply because they want to know who they are and where they come from, a foundational human need that non adopted people take for granted. Adopted people have begun to speak out against this discrimination. They ask: who do sealed birth certificates actually protect and serve?

The legislation which sealed original birth certificates never codified or even touched upon birth parent confidentiality, which many

Ami Dressen, left, and Illinois state representative Sara Feigenholtz, both adoptees, hold their original birth certificates. They are two of nearly nine thousand Illinois adoptees who have obtained their birth records through a new law sponsored by Feigenholtz.

Most Adopted Adolescents Have Contact with Their Birth Mothers and Most of Them Are Satisfied with the Contact

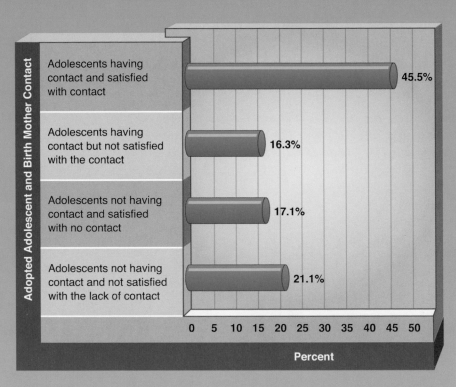

Adopted adolescents' expressions of satisfaction with their contact with their birth mother

Adopted Adolescent and Birth Mother Contact

- Adolescents having contact and satisfied with contact — 45.5%
- Adolescents having contact but not satisfied with the contact — 16.3%
- Adolescents not having contact and satisfied with no contact — 17.1%
- Adolescents not having contact and not satisfied with the lack of contact — 21.1%

0 5 10 15 20 25 30 35 40 45 50

Percent

Taken from: University of Massachusetts Psychology Department MN/TX Adoption Project. "Key Findings: Relationships Within the Adoption Kinship Network," 2008.

legislators believe was promised to these parents as a condition of surrender. Recent research conducted by Professor Elizabeth Samuels of the Baltimore School of Law, entitled "The Idea of Adoption: An Inquiry into the History of Adult Adoptees Access to Birth Records" which was published in the *Rutgers Law Review*, concludes that laws closing records to the parties were not enacted as a shield to protect birth parents, but rather as a sword to prevent them interfering with adoptive families.

The confidentiality of birth/natural parents has been a bone of contention in the struggle for adoptee rights and has been used as a smokescreen for other reasons to object to legislative reform. It is said for example that adoptive parents desire to keep the status quo. However, a 1997 study by Cornell University found adoptive parents overwhelmingly support adoptees' right to know. It is not surprising to find that there are adoptive parent legislators who support reform.

Many unproven fears retard the movement to grant adult adopted people their birthright. Some fear an increase in abortions, some fear a decline in adoption placements, some say birth mothers were given confidentiality. None of these fears have been justified in the histories of those states which have opened their records. Abortions have not increased. Adoptions have not decreased. These days a small percentage of birth mothers reject contact with their children. At the time of surrender, they signed only a surrender paper terminating their parental rights and confidentiality was not given. In any event, advocates say that those who are the most concerned, namely adopted people themselves, should have the same right to access their original birth certificates as everyone else. They should decide, without interference from the state.

A comprehensive study conducted in November 2007 by the Evan B. Donaldson Adoption Institute, the foremost think tank on adoption issues, concluded that adoptees behave with maturity and respect when contacting members of their natural families; the lives [of] natural/birth parents have not been ruined. This report urges all states to open their adoption records. A follow up study by the Donaldson Institute was released in 2010. . . .

Adopted Persons Are Speaking Out

Times have changed and thousands of adoptees and birth/natural parents search for each other every year. Several states have pending legislation and several states have partial open records, meaning adopted people born in certain years have access. Do birth/natural parents have access? Four states have enacted laws giving them search assistance, but not access. These are Hawaii, Illinois, Georgia and Tennessee.

The August 2012 protest in Chicago, Illinois organized by members of the Adoptee Rights Demonstration is a demand for legislators to vote on Adoptee Rights legislation, not to table it or to assign it to a committee known as "hell where bills go to die." Protesters are asking legislators to think hard about an adoptee's inalienable right to original identity and their need to know. Advocates describe sealed records laws as unfair, discriminatory and unenlightened, as relics of the past. Legislative change has been exceedingly slow and painstakingly difficult. It is past time for our laws [to] reflect current research, the norms of the civilized world and to recognize the full humanity of adopted persons!

EVALUATING THE AUTHOR'S ARGUMENTS:

What evidence do authors David Phelps and Joyce Bahr use to support their viewpoint? Do you think the evidence was strong, weak, or somewhere in the middle? Explain.

Laws Requiring Open Adoption Records Are Unwise

"A healthy culture of adoption requires that each individual participant has the rights to choose which parts of her adoption story to share, whom to share it with, and at what time."

Megan Lindsey

In the following viewpoint Megan Lindsey of the National Council for Adoption (NCFA) maintains that open records laws are unwise and unnecessary. According to Lindsey, the vast majority of adoptions today are open. This is a good thing, she asserts. It illustrates the acceptance and celebration of adoption as a positive outcome. As a result, says Lindsey, the number of sealed adoption records is subsiding. However, she says, there are still a small number of birth parents who want to maintain confidentiality and keep their adoption records closed. The NCFA, says Lindsey, supports these birth parents and opposes laws that require the opening of adoption records. Lindsey is an assistant director of policy at the NCFA, a nonprofit adoption organization.

Since 1980, the National Council For Adoption (NCFA) has worked to strengthen the culture of adoption in the U.S. and around the world. American society has come to recognize and honor adoption as a means of serving the best interests of children, birthparents, adoptive families, and society at large. While there is always room for improvement, it speaks positively of Americans' views and knowledge of adoption that adoption practices have become increasingly open and less secretive over time, minimizing the inappropriate connotation that adoption is ever, in any way, a shameful process.

A society that openly accepts and respects the positive practice of adoption allows all individuals who are part of the "adoption triad"— adopted individuals, birthparents, and adoptive parents—to feel accepted and validated if and when they choose to share their adoption stories with others, or when they decide to seek out more information about their own adoption stories. It is equally important that all members of the adoption triad and the public at large be equally accepting in those less frequent cases when an adopted individual or birthparent prefers to keep all or part of his adoption story confidential. A healthy culture of adoption requires that each individual participant has the right to choose which parts of her adoption story to share, whom to share it with, and at what time. It should also be her decision whether and when to seek previously undisclosed details about her adoption. Similarly, if confidentiality has been promised and remains desirable to any adopted individual or birthparent, it should be within their power to maintain it.

The debate over who should have access to original birth and adoption records, and when they should have it, is many-layered and often fraught with emotion on all sides. This article examines ways in which state laws, the adoption community, and the public can best honor the wishes of those seeking information and/or contact while also maintaining the right to privacy for those who desire it. If we expand this often contentious conversation—taking a less narrow and divisive approach to the issue of sharing information and reuniting birth-parents and adoptees—it is possible to pursue solutions that benefit everyone.

History of Birth Records and Information Sharing

Adoption practices have evolved significantly over time. Historically, there was a period in this country when adoption was unfairly viewed as something best kept secret. Unintended pregnancies and parenting outside of marriage both carried a far greater stigma than they do today, and infertility was also viewed less sympathetically. As a result, birthparents, adoptive parents, and adopted individuals often faced public censure or judgment, and adoption was viewed as a last resort rather than a positive option for children and families. In the vast majority of these past cases, despite facing an inappropriate and unfair cultural stigma, members of the adoption triad most likely had good intentions—birthparents choosing the option of adoption frequently did so in order to secure their child's future, and many adoptive parents seeking to build a family provided safe, loving environments for their children. While adoption practice and counseling has by necessity changed a great deal—and for the better—it is reasonable to believe that, on the whole, adoption professionals in the past sought to serve the interests of children and families as best they could.

> **FAST FACT**
>
> According to the US Department of Health and Human Services Child Welfare Information Gateway, approximately twenty-five states require adopted persons to obtain a court order to gain access to their original birth certificates.

Americans' Attitudes About Searching for Birth Parents: Impact on Birth Parents, 1997 and 2002

Question: "Sometimes people who were adopted as children look for and find one or both of the parents who placed them for adoption. When this happens, is this usually a good thing or bad thing for the parents who place them for adoption?"

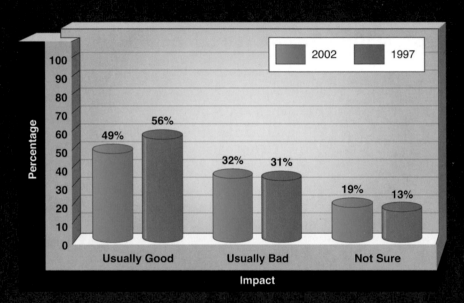

Taken from: Dave Thomas Foundation for Adoption. National Adoption Attitudes Survey, June 2002.

Early 20th-century adoption practices often sought to maintain the confidentiality of birthparents, due to both the stigma attached to adoption and the belief of many adoption practitioners that confidentiality would encourage attachment between children and their adoptive families. Unfortunately, practices promoting confidentiality also tended to perpetuate the perception of adoption as something shameful. Both practice and laws built a system that established confidentiality as the norm in adoption. In 1916, New York enacted the first law in the U.S. sealing adoption records from the public, and in 1917, Minnesota enacted a law sealing records from inspection by adult adoptees and birthparents as well as the general public. By the 1950s, the vast majority of states had sealed adoption records, and most had already implemented a system that created new birth certificates listing only a child's adoptive parents. These birth certificates provided legal documents of parentage to adoptive families while concealing the identities of birthparents and adopted individuals from one another and from the public.

Today adoption is far more widely accepted and celebrated as the positive outcome it is for birthparents, children, and adoptive families. Over time, this positive shift in cultural perception has led to more open adoption practices in a majority of U.S. cases. However, confidentiality (or more limited openness options that allow for the possibility of anonymity) remains important to a small number of participants, including some prospective birthparents. A recent survey questioned 100 private agencies from across the United States about the levels of openness in the adoptions they had facilitated during a two-year period; of the 4,400 adoptions facilitated by reporting adoption service providers, 5% (approximately 220) were confidential adoptions. If this same percentage were analogously applied to the approximately 18,078 adoptions facilitated annually nationwide we would see that approximately 904 adoption triads choose to participate in a confidential adoption each year.

While a clear majority of adoptions today contain some level of openness, and NCFA believes that this is a good trend, a choice made in one out of every twenty adoptions should not be discounted. If 5% of adoptions today are confidential upon the mutual agreement of adoption parties, then it is probable that a much higher percentage of individuals involved in past adoptions may well have desired confidentiality in part because open adoptions were less widely accepted.

Birth Records and Information Sharing Today

Given that a great and increasing majority of domestic adoptions today are open to some degree, and that best practice now requires birthparents to share, at minimum, medical and social background information with the adoptive family and adopted individual, the debate over birth records and information sharing has and will continue to subside. In domestic adoptions today, adoption professionals

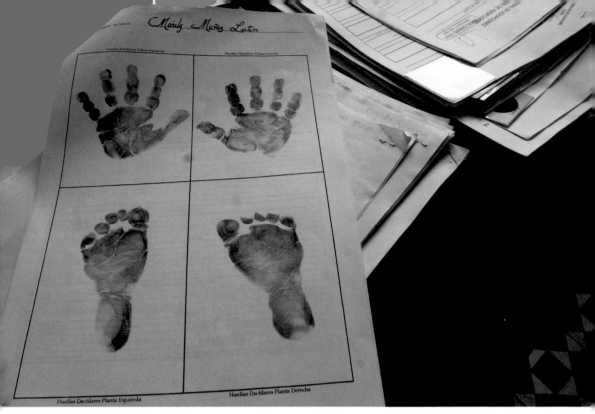

The best domestic adoption practices today require birth parents to share medical and social background information with the adoptive family and the adopted individual.

recommend that contact preferences be determined prospectively—at the time of an adoptive placement—while allowing for some future flexibility, as an individual's preferences may change over time.

Although total confidentiality in adoption has become far less common, some participants still prefer confidential adoption or a lesser degree of openness, which may include sharing only minimal information or communicating on very limited terms. Still, the trend towards openness is clear. In a recent study measuring levels of openness, birthparents and adoptive parents were interviewed and asked to report on the level of openness in their adoptions. The spectrum included a continuum of openness with seven openness descriptors. Adoptions described as "very closed" and "closed" were reported at 6% or less amongst the groups of reporting parents, showing that the vast majority of adoptions today have some level of openness.

The NCFA's Position

Over time, as open and semi-open adoptions have become the norm, there has also been an increasing amount of interest in exchanging information or facilitating reunions between birthparents and adopted individuals. Likewise, over time, NCFA's position has come to encompass the need for accommodation and compromise on the issues of information exchange, search, and reunion.

Absolutist advocates for open records claim that NCFA has always been and continues to be anti-reunion and anti-information sharing. This is untrue. NCFA has never opposed adoption reunions or information sharing, and in fact both accepts and encourages these outcomes for willing parties. Since our founding in 1980, NCFA has counted amongst our membership many adoption service providers that facilitate open adoption. We fully support reunions and the exchange of identifying information between members of the adoption triad when the parties themselves wish for such an exchange.

On rare occasions, a party to adoption may feel compelled to seek and later maintain his or her confidentiality. In these instances, NCFA encourages the keeping of past promises, while still satisfying those seeking information to the greatest extent possible and acceptable to the other party (or parties). This position of compromise is one NCFA has advocated throughout its history. NCFA's first president, William Pierce, was once quoted as saying, "I don't think open records are fair, but I don't think closed records are fair either." As former NCFA president Thomas Atwood later explained, "NCFA does not oppose reunions or the exchange of identifying information between mutually consenting parties to adoption. What we oppose is the law empowering one party to adoption to force himself or herself on another."

EVALUATING THE AUTHOR'S ARGUMENTS:

In this viewpoint the National Council for Adoption opposes opening all records, while the authors of the previous viewpoint want records opened. Identify the main reason each author provides for why they believe their viewpoint is correct. Which of these reasons do you think is more compelling, and why?

Facts About Adoption

Editor's note: These facts can be used in reports to add credibility when making important points or claims.

The following facts are from the 2007 National Survey of Adoptive Parents sponsored by the US Department of Health and Human Services.

Facts About US Adoptions
- Thirty-eight percent are private US adoptions.
- Thirty-seven percent are foster care adoptions.
- Twenty-five percent are international adoptions.

Facts About Adopted Children
- Forty-three percent lived with their birth families at some time prior to their adoption.
- Thirty-two percent were adopted at birth or were not yet one month old when placed with their adoptive parents.
- Twenty-four percent were adopted by relatives.
- Thirty-seven percent are non-Hispanic white.
- Forty percent are of a different race, culture, or ethnicity than both of their adoptive parents (or their sole parent if there is only one parent in the household).
- Six percent have a parent who was himself or herself adopted.
- Fourteen percent are under five years old.
- Twelve percent live in households with incomes below the poverty threshold.
- Thirty-nine percent have special health-care needs.
- Forty-nine percent are male.

Facts About Children Adopted from Other Countries
- Thirty-three percent were adopted from China.
- Thirteen percent were adopted from Russia.
- Eleven percent were adopted from Guatemala.
- Eleven percent were adopted from South Korea.
- Thirty-three percent are male.

Facts About Adopted Children's Mental and Behavioral Health Issues

- Twelve percent have been diagnosed with attachment disorder.
- Fourteen percent aged six or older have been diagnosed with attention deficit disorder or attention deficit/hyperactivity disorder (ADD/ADHD) and have parents who rated the condition as moderate or severe.
- Eight percent aged two or older have moderate or severe behavior or conduct problems, according to their parents.
- Two percent have been diagnosed with depression and have symptoms that are moderate or severe, according to their parents.
- Fourteen percent have problems with social behaviors, according to their parents.
- Eighty-eight percent have parents who report that they exhibit positive social behaviors.

Facts About Adoptive Parents

- Seventy-three percent are non-Hispanic white.
- Eighty-one percent report that the reason they adopted was to provide a permanent home for a child in need.
- Sixty-nine percent report that the reason they adopted was a desire to expand their family.
- Fifty-two percent report that the reason they adopted was an inability to have a biological child.
- Twenty-four percent report that the reason they adopted was to provide a sibling for another child.

Facts About Adoptive Parent and Child Relationships

- Eighty-one percent of adopted children have parents who report their relationship with their child as very warm and close.
- Forty-two percent of adopted children have parents who report the relationship as "better than ever expected."
- Fifteen percent of adopted children have parents who report the relationship as "more difficult than they ever expected."
- Eighty-seven percent of adopted children have parents who say they would "definitely" make the same decision to adopt their child.
- Three percent of adopted children have parents who say that they "probably would not" or "definitely would not" make the same decision to adopt their child.

Facts About Adoption Openness

- Ninety-seven percent of adopted children are aware they were adopted.
- Sixty-eight percent of privately adopted US children have had contact with their birth families.
- Thirty-nine percent of children adopted from foster care have had contact with their birth families.
- Six percent of children adopted internationally have had contact with their birth families.

Facts About the Costs of Adoption

- Twenty-nine percent of all adoptions had no cost.
- Twenty-three percent of all adoptions cost less than five thousand dollars.
- Nine percent of all adoptions cost more than five thousand dollars but less than ten thousand dollars.
- Thirty-nine percent of all adoptions cost ten thousand dollars or more.
- Forty-nine percent of international adoptions cost twenty thousand dollars or more.

Organizations to Contact

The editors have compiled the following list of organizations concerned with the issues debated in this book. The descriptions are derived from materials provided by the organizations. All have publications or information available for interested readers. The list was compiled on the date of publication of the present volume; the information provided here may change. Be aware that many organizations take several weeks or longer to respond to inquiries, so allow as much time as possible for the receipt of requested materials.

Administration for Children and Families (ACF)
370 L'Enfant Promenade SW
Washington, DC 20447
(202) 401-9200
website: www.acf.hhs.gov

The ACF is an agency within the US Department of Health and Human Services that partners with federal, state, tribal, and local agencies to improve the overall health and well-being of our nation's children and families. The Children's Bureau, within the ACF, provides reports and statistics on adoption in the United States, including annual reports from Child Welfare Outcomes Data and the Adoption and Foster Care Analysis and Reporting System. The Children's Bureau also provides funding for the AdoptUSKids project, which raises awareness about the adoption of children in foster care.

Adoption Exchange Association (AEA)
605 Global Way, Ste. 100
Linthicum, MD 21090
(410) 636-7030
fax: (888) 200-4005
e-mail: www.adoptea.org/contactus.html
website: www.adoptea.org

The AEA is a national nonprofit organization committed to the adoption of waiting children. AEA members are local, state, or regional adoption exchanges, which provide information about children waiting for adoptive families. The association is also the lead agency in the AdoptUSKids project to recruit adoptive families for children waiting in foster care across the United States. The AEA sponsors a yearly conference to facilitate the sharing of information between member adoption exchanges. The association publishes a monthly newsletter, the *AEA Membership News.*

Adoption Healing
74 Takewood Dr.
Congers, NY 10920-1710
(845) 268-0283
e-mail: info@AdoptionHealing.com
website: www.adoptionhealing.com

Adoption Healing is a nonprofit organization with a worldwide network committed to helping people who have been separated by adoption find each other. The organization seeks to preserve families, open adoption records, and educate the public about adoption-related issues. Adoption Healing provides adoption-related literature, support groups, healing weekends, conferences, and a nightly chat.

AdoptUSKids
605 Global Way, Ste. 100
Linthicum, MD 21090
(888) 200-4005
e-mail: info@adoptuskids.org
website: www.adoptuskids.org

AdoptUSKids is a multifaceted, federally funded project whose mission is to raise public awareness about the need for families for children in foster care and to assist states, territories, and tribes to recruit and retain foster and adoptive families and connect them with children. AdoptUSKids offers an array of services to both families and child welfare professionals and maintains an extensive database of children in US foster care available for adoption, as well as families who are home studied, approved, and ready to adopt them.

American Adoption Congress (AAC)
(202) 483-3399
e-mail: www.americanadoptioncongress.org/contact.php
website: www.americanadoptioncongress.org

The AAC is made up of individuals, families, and organizations that support adoption reform. The AAC is committed to increasing public awareness about the realities of adopted life for birth and adoptive families; changing public policies related to adoption practices in order to acknowledge adoption as an extension of family; enacting legislation in all states that guarantees access to identifying information for all adopted persons and their birth and adoptive families through records access and preservation of open adoption agreements; and facilitating birth family reunification for all adopted adults, without prior restraint, through search and support group networking and/or social service assistance. The AAC offers a quarterly publication, *Decree,* as well as the *Beacon*, a monthly newsletter.

Congressional Coalition on Adoption Institute (CCAI)
311 Massachusetts Ave. NE
Washington, DC 20002
(202) 544-8500
fax: (202) 544-8501
e-mail: info@ccainstitute.org
website: www.ccainstitute.org

The CCAI is a nonprofit organization that works to raise awareness about the needs of children without families and to remove policy barriers that hinder children from knowing the love and support a family provides. CCAI seeks to bring together policy makers and individuals with direct foster care or adoption experience in order to bring about legislative improvements in an effort to ensure each child has his or her right to a family realized. The institute publishes a newsletter several times during the year and provides many reports and fact sheets on adoption.

Dave Thomas Foundation for Adoption
716 Mt. Airyshire Blvd., Ste. 100
Columbus, OH 43235
(800) 275-3832
fax: (614) 764-3077
e-mail: info@davethomasfoundation.org
website: www.davethomasfoundation.org

The Dave Thomas Foundation for Adoption, established by the founder of the Wendy's fast-food chain, believes that every child deserves to live in a safe, loving, and permanent family; no child should linger in foster care or leave the system at age eighteen without a permanent family of his or her own; and every child is adoptable. The foundation works to find homes for children who are waiting to be adopted from foster care and to educate adults about foster care adoption. The organization raises money to provide free educational resources, promote awareness, assist policy makers and employers, and support adoption professionals and agencies throughout the United States and Canada. The foundation provides several guides and facts sheets, including *Finding Forever Families: A Step-by-Step Guide to Adoption* and *A Step-by-Step Guide to Post-Adoption.*

Evan B. Donaldson Adoption Institute
120 E. Thirty-Eighth St.
New York, NY 10016
(212) 925-4089
fax: (775) 796-6592
e-mail: info@adoptioninstitute.org
website: www.adoptioninstitute.org

The Evan B. Donaldson Adoption Institute's mission is to provide leadership that improves adoption laws, policies, and practices in order to better the lives of everyone touched by adoption. The institute conducts and synthesizes research, offers education to inform public opinion, promotes ethical practices and legal reforms, and works to translate policy into action. The institute sponsors many programs, projects, conferences, and events. It also provides many books and publications, including the *Adoption Institute E-newsletter.*

National Adoption Center (NAC)
1500 Walnut St., Ste. 701
Philadelphia, PA 19102
(800) 862-3678
e-mail: nac@adopt.org
website: www.adopt.org

The mission of the NAC is to expand adoption opportunities for children living in foster care throughout the United States and to be a resource for families and agencies who seek caring homes for children. The NAC operates a website, Wednesday's Child, which profiles children available for adoption in Atlanta, Los Angeles, New York, Philadelphia, and metropolitan Washington, D.C. The NAC also sponsors several online communities where professionals, potential adopters, judges, legislators, birth parents, adoptees, and others with an interest in adoption can share information and communicate with each other.

National Council for Adoption (NCA)
225 N. Washington St.
Alexandria, VA 22314-2561
(703) 299-6633
fax: (703) 299-6004
e-mail: ncfa@adoptioncouncil.org
website: www.adoptioncouncil.org

The NCA is a nonprofit organization that advocates for adoption through education, research, and legislative action. The organization focuses on infant adoption, adoption out of foster care, and intercountry adoption. The NCF serves children, birth parents, adoptive families, adult adoptees, adoption agencies, US and foreign governments, policy makers, the media, and the general public as a voice for adoption. The organization's monthly publication, the *Adoption Advocate*, provides information on child welfare and adoption issues.

For Further Reading

Books

Carangelo, Lori. *Chosen Children*. Palm Desert, CA: Access, 2011. The author is the founder of the organization Americans for Open Records. In this self-published book, she contends that adopted children are overrepresented in the nation's prisons and psychiatric hospitals. She provides data and a multitude of stories on failed adoptions, people harmed by adoption, and people wanting to be reunited with their biological parents.

Cogen, Patty. *Parenting Your Internationally Adopted Child: From Your First Hours Together Through the Teen Years*. Cambridge, MA: Harvard Common, 2008. In this book, child and family therapist Patty Cogen provides a guide to parents adopting internationally. She explains how adoptive parents can help their adopted child bond with them and become part of the family. She also describes how to help internationally adopted children develop a positive self-image that incorporates both their new American identity and their ethnic origins.

Crumpacker, Bunny, and J.S. Picariello. *Jessica Lost: A Story of Birth, Adoption & the Meaning of Motherhood*. New York: Union Square, 2011. This book chronicles two stories. First, it provides the story of a middle-aged woman adopted as an infant who begins to search for her birth mother. Second, it provides the story of the woman's birth mother and her heartrending decision to give her daughter up for adoption. The voices and stories of each of the women are intertwined in the book as their search to find each other and to fill the emptiness in their lives is chronicled.

Douglas, Anthony, and Terry Philpot, eds. *Adoption: Changing Families, Changing Times*. New York: Routledge, 2004. This book is a compilation of viewpoints from those with an interest in adoption, including adopted children and adults, birth parents, adoptive parents, those who work in the adoption field, educators, and policy makers. The book covers children and young people in foster care, trying to adopt, waiting for adoption, life after adoption, the politics of adoption, and other topics.

Eldridge, Sherri. *Questions Adoptees Are Asking*. Colorado Springs, CO: NavPress, 2009. The author interviewed more than seventy adoptees to find the questions they all have in common, such as "Does my birth mother ever think about me?" and "Was I a mistake?" As she pieces together these common questions, Eldridge helps adoptees understand that they are not alone and helps adoptive parents understand the inner lives of adoptees.

Fessler, Ann. *The Girls Who Went Away*. New York: Penguin, 2007. Adoptee Ann Fessler provides a view into the culture of adoption and unwed mothers in America between 1945 and 1973, before abortion was legalized. Fessler interviewed more than one hundred women who were pressured to surrender their children for adoption during this time. Fessler's mother was one of these women.

Gelles, Richard J. *The Book of David: How Preserving Families Can Cost Children's Lives*. New York: Basic, 1997. The author, a sociologist and expert on family violence, uses the tragic story of a murdered child to argue that the child welfare system must be changed so that children are not left in troubled families for the sake of family preservation. David Edwards was murdered by his mother after he fell through the cracks in the child welfare system. Gelles contends that if David's protection was considered first and foremost above family preservation, the child's life may have been spared.

Harrison, Kathy. *Another Place at the Table*. New York: Tarcher, 2004. In this book, Harrison provides a real-life glimpse of the US foster care system, the troubled children in the system who need homes, and what it is like to be a foster parent and an adoptive parent. For many years Harrison was a hotline foster parent, one who could be relied on to foster children in emergency situations. During her time as a foster parent, Harrison fostered abandoned babies, runaway teens, preschoolers with disabilities, and children with psychiatric disorders.

Joyce, Kathryn. *The Child Catchers: Rescue, Trafficking, and the New Gospel of Adoption*. New York: Public Affairs, 2013. This book is an exposé on the US evangelical adoption movement, which urges women to choose adoption. According to the author, anyone who seeks to adopt is affected by the evangelical adoption movement, whether they know it or not. The movement has shaped the way people think about adoption, the language used to discuss it, the places from which people adopt, and the policies and laws that govern the process. Joyce provides real-life stories of those caught up in the profit-driven adoption industry.

Lifton, Betty Jean. *Lost and Found: The Adoption Experience*. Ann Arbor: University of Michigan Press, 2009. This is an updated and expanded edition of *Lost and Found*, which the late author originally published in 1979. Lifton was a writer, adoptee, and adoption reform advocate. Since the original publication of the book, it has been essential reading for anyone wanting to understand adoption from the perspective of the child, the birth mother, and the adoptive mother. This updated edition provides new material on the controversies surrounding adoption.

Pavao, Joyce Maguire. *The Family of Adoption*. Boston, MA: Beacon, 2005. Family and adoption therapist Joyce Maguire Pavao describes the different stages of adoption that she contends all adopted children must go through. These stages include feelings of loss, school problems, and a desire to learn about their past. Pavao uses real adoption stories to explain why adoptive parents must understand these stages and be open with their adopted children.

Rhodes-Courter, Ashley. *Three Little Words: A Memoir*. New York: Atheneum Books for Young Readers, 2009. In this book, a young woman describes growing up and surviving in the American foster care system before finally finding a permanent and stable family. Rhodes-Courter conveys the distress of being removed from her mother's care and trying to cling to her despite her instability and unpredictability. In the foster care system, Rhodes-Courter would face other troubles, including living in fourteen different foster homes—some of which were abusive—and being shuffled between caseworkers and schools. After nearly ten years in the system, she was eventually adopted and now tries to help other foster care children.

Trenka, Jane Jeong, Julia Chinyere Oparah, and Sun Yung Shin, eds. *Outsiders Within*. Cambridge, MA: South End, 2006. The editors have compiled studies, personal essays, poems, and artwork from transracial adoptees around the world. The compiled works reveal the emotional, cultural, and economic difficulties of transracial adoption, as well as its benefits.

Periodicals and Internet Sources

Allen, Candice. "Finding Your Family: For a Number of Air Force Reservists, Adoption Is the Best Option," *Citizen Airman*, December 2012.

Apodaca, Rose. "The Truth and Lies About Adoption," *Harper's Bazaar*, February 23, 2012.

Barnett, Melanie. "Chinese-Born, American-Made: Melanie Barnett's Birth Parents Could Keep Only One of Their Newborn Twins. They Chose Her Brother, and Her Long Journey Began," *New York Times Upfront*, January 2, 2012.

Bartholet, Elizabeth. "International Adoption: The Human Rights Position," *Global Policy*, January 2010.

Brown, Kim. "The Past and the Future of International Adoption: An Expert's Opinions and Experiences," *Adoption Voices Magazine*, April 12, 2012. http://adoptionvoicesmagazine.com/expert-con nection/the-past-and-the-future-of-international-adoption-an-ex perts-opinions-and-experiences-2.

Callahan, Nicole Soojung. "What to Expect When You're . . . Adopted," *Slate*, April 23, 2013. www.slate.com/articles/double_x /doublex/2013/04/when_an_adoptee_gets_pregnant_the_desire _to_find_her_birth_family_gets_stronger.html?wpisrc=newsletter _jcr:content.

Crary, David. "Open Adoption: New Report Details Increase," *Huffington Post*, March 21, 2012. www.huffingtonpost .com/2012/03/21/open-adoption-increase_n_1371122.html.

Daily Beast. "Solutions for the Adoption Crisis," November 17, 2010. www.thedailybeast.com/articles/2010/11/17/international-adop tion-fixing-local-and-foreign-orphanages.html.

Day, Nicholas. "The U.S. Children's Bureau: Parenting Advice from Uncle Sam," *Slate*, April 23, 2013. www.slate.com/blogs/how _babies_work/2013/04/23/history_of_parenting_advice_the_u_s _children_s_bureau.html?wpisrc=newsletter_jcr:content.

Gates, Gary J. "Family Formation and Raising Children Among Same-Sex Couples," *National Council on Family Relations; Family Focus on . . . LGBT Families*, Winter 2011. http://williamsinstitute .law.ucla.edu/wp-content/uploads/Gates-Badgett-NCFR-LGBT -Families-December-2011.pdf.

Gilmore, Jennifer. "The Long Wait," *Vogue*, October 2012.

Graham, Jennifer. "When Adoptions Fail," *Boston Globe*, June 18, 2012. www.bostonglobe.com/opinion/2012/06/17/graham /tmPXOPHJup4ScQPacoASpL/story.html.

Inskeep, Steve. "Modern Family," *Newsweek*, February 15, 2013.

Lutz, Lisa. "Meet the Parents," *New York Times Magazine*, May 6, 2012.

Mears, Bill. "High Court to Tackle Native American Adoption Dispute," CNN, January 4, 2012. www.cnn.com/2013/01/04 /justice/native-american-adoption-dispute/index.html?hpt=hp_t2.

Monika. "What Is Open Adoption: One Birthmom's Perspective," *Give1Save1* (blog), August 2, 2012. http://give1save1domestic .blogspot.com/2012/08/what-is-open-adoption-one-birthmoms .html.

Mother & Baby. "'She Chose Us Rather than the Other Way Around!,'" July 4, 2012.

Murphy, Rhona. "Light in the Heart of Darkness," *Newsweek*, January 16, 2012.

Park, Madison. "Russian Lawmakers Eye Adoption Ban to US," CNN, December 27, 2012. www.cnn.com/2012/12/19/world /russia-adoption-u-s-ban/index.html?hpt=hp_t3.

Parsons, Sabrina. "Working Women: When Have You Waited Too Long to Become a Mom?," *Forbes*, October 3, 2011. www.forbes .com/sites/sabrinaparsons/2011/10/03/working-women-when -have-you-waited-too-long-to-become-a-mom.

Ponnuru, Ramesh. "Marriage and Adoption: Traditionalists Do Not Slight the Latter," *National Review*, May 6, 2013.

Powers, Ann. "Sharing Rebecca: A Mother's Story of Her Daughter's Open Adoption," *Parenting*, December 29, 2011. www.parenting .com/article/open-adoption.

Spear, Nicole. "Adopted Children's Outcomes as Young Adults in Regards to Educational Attainment and Income," *Park Place Economist*, 2009.

Sullivan, Laura, and Amy Walters. "Native Foster Care: Lost Children, Shattered Families," NPR, October 25, 2011. www.npr.org/series/141763531/native-foster-care-lost-children-shattered-families.

Walker, Ken. "Opening the Adoption Files: Secrecy Gives Way to Relationships with Birth Mothers," *Christianity Today*, October 2012.

Wardle, Connie. "'Unfit Mother' Speaks Up: Church Should Better Understand the Pain of Adoption, Former Armagh Resident Says," *Presbyterian Record*, June 2012.

Watson, Rob. "Foster Care Adoption: The 5 Reasons Why You Don't Want to Do It, and the 5 Greater Reasons Why You Do," *Huffington Post*, November 19, 2012. www.huffingtonpost.com/rob-watson/foster-care-adoption_b_2155329.html.

Weller, Sheila, and Mariska Hargitay. "My Faith Pulled Me Through," *Good Housekeeping*, May 2012.

White, Rachel R. "I Was Sold as a Baby for Thousands of Dollars," *Cosmopolitan*, September 2012.

Young, Cathy. "Putin's Innocent Victims: A Mean-Hearted Ban on the Adoption of Russian Children by American Parents," *Weekly Standard*, February 4, 2013.

Zweifel, Julianne E., Sharon N. Covington, and Linda D. Applegarth. "'Last-Chance Kids': A Good Deal for Older Parents—but What About the Children?," *SRM*, May 2012. www.srm-ejournal.com/article.asp?AID=10433.

Index

on lack of energy as disadvantage of parenthood after age 40, 66

on percentage of white *vs.* nonwhite same-sex couples having adopted child, *45*

on searching for birth parents, *106*

of state welfare agencies on impact of ICWA on children remaining in foster care, *80*

See also specific surveys

T

The Idea of Adoption (Samuels), 100

Today Show (TV program), 85

Transracial adoption(s)

percentages of, adoption type, *51*

should be encouraged, 48–52

should not be encouraged, 53–57

U

United Kingdom

opening of adoption records in, 98

percentages of black *vs.* white children adopted from government care in, *56*

promotion of transracial adoption in, 54–55

Urban Institute, 36

W

Wendy's Wonderful Kids (WWK) program, 8–9

Western Journal of Nursing Research, 17

Williams Institute, 36

Wolf, Judy, 62–64

WWK (Wendy's Wonderful Kids) program, 8–9

Y

Young, Kit, *95*

Z

Zeanah, Charles, 19

Zug, Marcia, 71

Picture Credits

© AP Images/Moises Castillo, 30, 108

© AP Images/The Charlotte Observer, Chris Keane, 70

© AP Images/Michel Euler, 44

© AP Images/Nam Y. Huh, 88

© AP Images/Chris Keane, 95

© AP Images/Seth Pearlman, 99

© AP Images/Tulsa World, James Gibbard, 73

© Aurora Photos/Alamy, 13, 49

© Catchlight Visual Services/Alamy, 68

© Cengage, Gale, 14, 20, 25, 32, 37, 46, 51, 56, 63, 67, 76, 80, 87, 93, 100, 106

© Enterline Design/Alamy, 10

© David Grossman/Alamy, 60

© Roadell Hickman/The Plain Dealer/Landov, 26

© MBI/Alamy, 18

© Ian Nicholson/PA Photos/Landov, 55

© The Photo Works/Alamy, 33

© Queerstock, Inc./Alamy, 39

© Stringer/Reuters/Landov, 82